SHAKESPEARE'S DOCTRINE OF NATURE

A STUDY OF *KING LEAR*

by the same author

★

ELIZABETHAN AND JACOBEAN POETS

SHAKESPEARE'S DOCTRINE OF NATURE

A STUDY OF *KING LEAR*

by

JOHN F. DANBY

FABER AND FABER
24 Russell Square
London

First published in mcmxlix *1949*
by Faber and Faber Limited
24 Russell Square London W.C.1
Second impression mcmli
Third impression mcmlviii
Fourth impression mcmlxi
Fifth impression mcmlxiv
Printed in Great Britain by
John Dickens & Co Ltd Northampton

To

MY FATHER AND MOTHER

ACKNOWLEDGMENTS

My debts in this book are extensive and of long standing. The oldest is to the Rev. Alan Eccleston, M.A., who is in one sense this book's only begetter, and who knew in the early 'thirties all I try to say now. Equally great is my debt to Dr. E. M. W. Tillyard and to Professor Basil Willey—both for original impulses into the field of Shakespeare study and English thought, and for kindly control and subsequent guidance of the impulses given. A great and indefinable deal I owe to Dr. J. Bronowski, mostly for his friendship, but also for his example.

I should also like to thank Professor G. Bullough, of King's College, London, and Mr. B. Colgrave, Reader in English, Durham University, whose encouragement and criticism came just at the right time; Mr. W. H. G. Armytage who has plied me with both encouragement and criticism all the time; and Helena M. Shire and David Shillan—whose help has been in the spirit if not in the letter.

My greatest debt is that which I owe to Gertrude, the best of instructors in the meaning of meaning: she will understand that this book is not even part-payment.

I also wish to thank the Editor of the *Durham University Journal* for permission to reprint, almost unchanged, an article which now constitutes Part II, Chapter II of this book.

J. F. D.

CONTENTS

11

CONTENTS

Part III

THE POET'S SOCIETY

PART I

THE TWO NATURES

[I]

THE CHRONICLE PLAY AND THE DRAMA OF IDEAS

We go to great writers for the truth. Or for whatever reason we go to them in the first place it is for the truth we return to them, again and again. What this truth is, both for the poetry which we call universal and for the criticism which tries to get at this truth, I propose to examine in Part III. The present section is by way of prologue only.

King Lear can be regarded as a play dramatizing the meanings of the single word 'Nature'. When looked at in this way it becomes obvious at once that *King Lear* is a drama of ideas—such a drama of ideas not as the Morality play had been, a drama of abstractions; nor such a drama of amusing talk about theses as Bernard Shaw's is; a drama of ideas, however, none the less, and Shakespeare's own creation: the real *Novum Organum* of Elizabethan thought.

The word 'Nature', as is well known, has several meanings. Romantic Nature, for example, is an invisible energy behind the things we see. For some of the Elizabethans, on the other hand, Nature means the visible creation regarded as an orderly arrangement. In the course of time 'Nature' changes its meaning. Furthermore, in any single period more than one meaning for the word may be current. And, most significant thing of all, some of these meanings will quarrel. They are so many rivals committed to an internecine struggle. Quarrels over what 'Nature' really means are not merely verbal: weapons will out as often as words. People identify themselves with the fate of their meaning. The quarrel might be a matter of life or death. Thus Giordano Bruno was imprisoned in 1593 and burnt in

15

1600. One reason for this was an unacceptable sense in which he used the word 'Nature'.

The sorts of meanings men die for are at least as real as the fires in which the same men burn, and the meanings of 'Nature' in which Shakespeare is interested are meanings of this sort. They are, I think, the moving parts of his world. They are the structural frames by which men live and work and think. A meaning is not a dictionary sense. It can be a programme of action. The human being who chooses such and such a meaning is deciding for such and such a course of behaviour among his fellows. The Inquisition will thus be forced to burn Giordano, and Giordano driven to die rather than recant.

The liberal tradition in the last century could not grasp this necessity for either inquisition or martyrdom over the question of a man's ideas. We nowadays are better placed. We see that an idea sometimes represents the life-interest of a group. It stands for a claim on society and a stake in reality. Both Marxist and moralist agree: one's ideas represent one's role as an agent among other agents. It is not necessary to imagine that the group does the thinking. It is only necessary to recognize that in the field of meaning ideas can be principles of action too. Conversely, bits of behaviour can have the force of ideas, implying a view of what man really is, and what kind of a world surrounds him. A goal towards which he must strive can be proposed. And such goals tend to exclusiveness. All man's goods are jealous goods.

Different views on Nature, therefore, are not differences of opinion only. They are felt as so many stubborn holds that reality has on us and we on it. They are such meanings as can become concrete people. People, in fact, feel themselves to be what they are only so long as these particular meanings hold good. They cling to them rather than to their lives. Such ideas, Coleridge would say, are not merely regulative but constitutive of our being.

Ideas can have, then, a political implication. What we think is in part conditioned by how we are placed. The clash of meaning in one's debating club is an intrusion from the world outside. Furthermore, an event completely unintellectual might radically affect a system of thought. The discovery of gunpowder, or banking, or America, seals the fate of ideas. The argument over the meaning of 'Nature' is one which the philosopher does not monopolize, nor are the meanings people will die for always settled or defined in terms of the philosopher's 'ideas'. Poor Tom, dispossessed daughter, Bastard son, rejected King—all these take their part, and not by ratiocination only, in the argument. Ideas are aspects of social action, competing and co-operating in a community of other ideas, among variegated groupings of interests and men.

A final thing might be noticed. It is something the moralist would add to the sociologist's account of ideas and group interests. In the moral sphere a man must act in accordance with his ideas, and in the course of action his ideas themselves will undergo development: new ideas suddenly occur, fresh insights are won. A man is in himself a society of meanings. It is because of this that he can choose. And it is by choice that he grows. The collision of ideas in the world of group-interests is paralleled by the competition of ideas in the realm of private choice. The great artist like Shakespeare takes both spheres of choice for his own. His art expresses and illuminates the field of choice. He takes the reflections of the philosopher and the actions of the unthinking man and explains the one to the other; and both he explains in terms of the central meaning which neither can monopolize, and which only art—such an art as Shakespeare's—can adequately present.

Drama is an especially apt vehicle for the handling of meanings. Meanings are always meanings-for-people. And people move among other people with their other ideas. Under the pressure of truth or circumstance one meaning can be adopted or another discarded. We watch the development of an idea and a man, people animating meanings and meanings animating people. Over the province of meaning which a play takes for its own we can watch the manifold inflections of the idea: in *King Lear*, the idea of Nature. *King Lear* consistently presents its characters choosing among the natures, basing themselves on the meaning they descry, acting according to the nature they elect. Even when they themselves are unaware of conscious choice we can recognize their bits of behaviour as animations of an idea.

Ideas as a part of persons, and persons as part of a process—in so describing human existence we are also describing the form of drama. Shakespearian drama is literally a new organ of thought. It is only dramatically that the manner of living thought can be adequately expressed. A discursive philosopher is tied to the script of his single part. The universal playwright, without self-contradiction, can include Hooker and Hobbes in the same play: as, I think, Shakespeare does in *King Lear*. There is a real sense in which *King Lear* incorporates the living parts of both *Ecclesiastical Polity* and *Leviathan*.

Elizabethan drama took an enormous stride in passing from the Morality to the kind of drama Shakespeare was writing. Without throwing aside Morality earnestness, or the Morality concern with abstract ideas, to these Shakespearian drama added flesh and blood: suspense, the tensions that beget and are begotten by choice, awareness of the passage of time, ability to portray growth. The change is momentous. The Morality could not depict process; it could only handle products. It could not suggest growth, the dynamic of ideas passing into and out of people; it could only present a thesis, and never got beyond its initial premise. The Morality is not an organ of thought as Shakespeare's Chronicle plays are.

By a sound instinct the Chronicle play gives its ideas to people and puts its people into a story. The ideas are thus planted where they can feed, be changed, and grow. The new form of the dramatized story is a new form of thought. The *dramatis personae* hold to whatever meanings they will abide by and the story propels them into action, towards a richer realization of what their thought implies.

The Elizabethan Playhouse is thus the true successor to the Medieval pulpit. At its best, Elizabethan drama handled human destiny as it had never been handled since the days of the preaching friar, or since Latimer and his Sermons of the Plough. The popularity of the Elizabethan drama might be explained by its religious content. In it the Elizabethan could see the everyday and temporal beside the unusual and eternal, 'the times' in a perspective of God and Magistrate. The preaching friar had disappeared. The official incumbent had to stick to the script of the official Homilies. A new religious form of thought, at once popular and serious, was essential. Only the drama could respond to the need. It is nice to fancy that this might explain the passage, within one generation, from something like *Cambises* to something as vast as *King Lear*.

Shakespeare, therefore, in *King Lear* does not maintain an abstract Morality thesis. Nothing, however, of the Morality thesis is lost. The real matter of morality is handled in terms of this new organ of thought—the Chronicle play. (*King Lear*, like *Henry VI*, is called a 'chronicle'.) Sometimes in speaking of the characters in the play it will be necessary to speak of them as if they were animated 'ideas'. This will do no harm if it is remembered that for us—and, I think, for Shakespeare—the ideas are such meanings as are also people, such ideas as can only be presented as the truth-interests of actual human beings. Shakespeare criticism has had enough experience of the 'symbol' and 'image' and 'theme' approach to be warned of the danger invited by too naïve a reaction against Bradley and common sense.

The words 'nature', 'natural', 'unnatural' occur over forty times in *King Lear*. This compares with twenty-five instances in *Timon of Athens* and twenty-eight in *Macbeth*. The expected range of the Elizabethan meanings of the word is covered. More significantly, however, two main meanings, strongly contrasted and mutually exclusive, run through the play. On one side is the view consciously adopted by Edmund, and tacitly assumed by Goneril and Regan. On the other is the view largely held by the Lear party. This latter is the traditional and orthodox view. Its limiting expression is Cordelia. To Cordelia, however, as standing for Nature herself, we propose to give separate consideration.

The view of the Lear party is the same as that found in Bacon and Hooker. Edmund's philosopher (just old enough in 1606 to have seen Edmund on the stage) is Hobbes. One part of the thought in *King Lear* we shall put alongside the similar contemporary expressions of Hooker and Bacon. Then we shall turn to the revolutionary view of Nature put forward by Edmund and seconded by Hobbes. Two poles of the play, from one point of view, are Edmund and Edgar. The aim of this chapter will be to understand what this polarity means—what that meaning is which forces the King from his kingdom, overturns his wits, destroys his daughter, and is only narrowly frustrated in the end by Edgar and human kindness.

[II]

THE BENIGNANT NATURE OF BACON, HOOKER, AND LEAR

Chaucer thought of Nature as a kindly Queen-motherly Dame. Since the mid-nineteenth century (and maybe more so since Hiroshima) we have come to think of Nature as a cruel and dangerously explosible force. The orthodox Elizabethans, for the most part, are nearer to the Chaucerian view. For us Nature is a source of raw power which we can use. If we are only clever enough we can make it serve our purposes. For the Elizabethans, on the other hand, Nature is an ordered and beautiful arrangement, to which we must adjust ourselves. Where we study Nature in order to exploit it, Bacon and Hooker study her in order to discover their duties. They think not of our controlling her but of allowing her to control us.

The idea of Nature, then, in orthodox Elizabethan thought, is always something normative for human beings. It is impossible to talk about Nature without talking also about pattern and ideal form; about Reason as displayed in Nature; about Law as the innermost expression of Nature; about Custom which is the basis of Law and equally with Law an expression of Nature's pattern; about Restraint as the observance of Law, and the way to discover our richest self-fulfilment. In the sixteenth century the forces which have produced our view of Nature were, of course, already at work. *King Lear* finds room in its world for the Nature which is no kindly Dame but the shattering power of Thunder. But the orthodox and benignant view is also strongly represented. It is the view of those in the play who seem already to be slightly old-fashioned, but who are nevertheless unquestionably the most human.

In the allegory of 'Pan, or Nature' Bacon gives the orthodox view fairly fully. Bacon is brisk and efficient. He always sounds like the new manager descending on the old firm. We hear the swish of his new broom, and are constantly surprised to recognize the familiar bric-a-brac cleaned up and offered as a new line. The allegory of Pan is a shop-window piece. It has every appearance of being an insertion into the *Advancement* from Bacon's commonplace book—a flight of fancy with which Bacon was particularly pleased:

The Fable is, perhaps, the noblest of all antiquity, and pregnant with the mysteries and secrets of nature. Pan, as the name imports, represents the universe, about whose origin there are two opinions; viz., that it either sprung from Mercury, that is, the Divine Word, according to the Scriptures and philosophical divines; or from the confused seeds of things. For some of the philosophers held that the seeds and elements of nature were infinite in their substance. . . . Others more accurately maintain that the variety of nature can equally spring from seeds, certain and definite in their substance, but only diversified in form and figure. . . . But others teach only one principle of nature—Thales,

water; Anaximenes, air; Heraclitus, fire. . . . They who introduced—
as Plato and Aristotle—primordial matter, every way disarranged,
shapeless, and indifferent to any form, approached nearer to a resem-
blance of the figure of the parable. For they conceived matter as a
courtezan, and the forms as suitors. . . . The third origin of Pan . . .
relates to the state of the world not in its first creation, but as made
subject to death and corruption after the fall; and in this state it was and
remains the offspring of God and Sin, or Jupiter and Reproach. (*Advancement of Learning*, Bk. II, Ch. 13.)

Bacon here summarizes the outstanding views on Nature—the
views of the Greek scientists and the Christian theologians—as he
understands them. First there is the theory that the universe
springs from the divine Logos; then the theory that places its
origins in matter—either as a collection of potentially infinite
seeds, or as a primordial substance capable of configuration
through its unions with form; finally the account of the universe since the fall—the secondary state of corruption after Sin
has taken a hand in the scheme made originally perfect by God.

The context in *King Lear* that immediately comes to mind is,
of course, Lear's cry to the Thunder:

> Crack nature's moulds, all germens spill at once
> That make ungrateful man. (III, ii.)

or his other outburst:

> Then let them anatomise Regan: see what breeds about her heart.
> Is there any cause in Nature that makes these hard hearts? (III, vi.)

The Thunder always tends to bring out Lear's heterodoxy.
Strict orthodoxy would reply to him that there is no cause in
Nature, except in that fallen nature which is the offspring of
Jupiter and Reproach. Neither the germens nor the original
copulations of matter with the forms can in themselves contain
the cause of ingratitude. Ingratitude is man-made. It enters
through the breach of nature made by Adam's sin. For the rest,
Shakespeare's thought seems to follow the second of Bacon's
theories. Lear's 'germens' are Bacon's 'seeds', his 'moulds'

Bacon's 'forms'. The sinister thing is the undertone—the suggestion that there is an explosive power that can smash the forms.

Even the suggestion of such a thought is a long way from Bacon's Pan. There is change and decay in his Nature, but always in the containing frame:

The Destinies are justly made Pan's sisters; for the rise, preservation, and dissolution of things: their depressions, exaltations, processes, triumphs, and whatever else can be ascribed to individual natures, are called fates and destinies. . . . Pan, or the nature of things, is the cause of these several changes and effects. . . . Horns are given him broad at the roots, but narrow and sharp a-top, because the nature of all things seems pyramidal: for individuals are infinite; but being collected into a variety of species, they rise up into kinds; and these again ascend, and are contracted into generals, till at length nature may seem collected to a point, which is signified by the pyramidal figure of Pan's horns. And no wonder if Pan's horns reach to the heavens, since the sublimities of nature, or abstract ideas, reach in a manner to things divine. Thus Homer's famous chain of natural causes is tied to the foot of Jupiter's chair; and indeed no-one can treat of metaphysics, or of the internal and immutable in nature, without rushing at once into natural theology.

Two points might be underlined in connection with this passage. First, Nature is a rational arrangement. Bacon, in fact, might be charged with making his account of Nature's internal structure almost crudely rational. Man's discourse of reason proceeds by abstraction from the particular to the general. Conveniently, as Bacon describes it, Nature works in the same way. Each rung of increased generality is reckoned a further degree of reality, until the limit of abstraction is reached and 'at length nature may seem contracted to a point'. There is a direct connection between man's logical order and the order of the physical universe.

The second point is equally important: Nature is not only a rational arrangement, but also a benevolent one. It has been arranged by God. If we observe it or think about it closely enough, it will conduct thought back to God: for 'No-one can treat of . . . the internal and immutable in nature, without rushing at once into natural theology'. Nature displays a wisdom, regularity, and beauty more than human in its devisal. As Lear says, thinking of the limitations of human skill, 'Nature's above Art in that respect'.

The idea of Nature's supreme art is one of Hooker's starting-points for the discussion of Nature in *Ecclesiastical Polity*. The following passage is introduced by the figure of Nature holding up 'some absolute shape or mirror' which she then takes as the model from which to copy the actual world:

> Yea, such her dexterity and skill appeareth, that no intellectual creature in the world were able by capacity to do that which nature doth without capacity and knowledge; it cannot be but nature hath some director of infinite knowledge to guide her in all her ways. Who the guide of nature, but only the God of nature? 'In him we live, move, and are.' Those things which nature is said to do, are by divine art performed, using nature as an instrument. (Bk. I, Ch. iii, 4.)

This brings us to the view that Nature is in some sense an ideal pattern. For both Bacon and Hooker, Nature is bound to God. The actual and the ideal, therefore, cannot be separated by too great a gulf. It may be that the 'absolute shape' cannot be directly beheld: the mirror is necessary, and our eye looking into the mirror might dim or distort. The 'absolute shape or mirror', however, which Nature studies as her model, is meant to explain the actual beauty and order of the work which confronts us in the world—the phenomena actually visible, tangible, recognizable.

The 'nature' of a thing is the stable pattern of its habits and qualities. As Nature is bound to God, man is bound to Nature. He, too, therefore has his 'absolute shape'—sadly impaired, in man's case, by man's own action. Man does not dress himself, as Fuller might say, by the ideal mirror. As we should say, in man's case the *forms* are only *norms*.

When Hooker thinks of Nature as rational arrangement he is not making Bacon's naïve hypostasis of the logical method. What he has in mind might best be explained by way of a contrast with our modern notions of natural law.

We think of natural law as exerting a kind of mechanical necessity. Mechanical necessity did not trouble the Elizabethans. The cosmos was not yet seen as a machine. Creatures did not emerge on an endless belt as products from a mass-production factory. Each creature, on the contrary, under God, was a self-maintaining 'this'. It was not part of a machine. Rather, it was an intelligence observing its rightful place in a community. What held it in place and held the community together was Reason. The law it observed was felt more as self-expression than as external restraint. It was a law, in any case, which the creature was most itself when it obeyed. And rebellion against this law was rebellion against one's self, loss of all nature, lapse into chaos. For us natural law is structure already decided on and laid down. Hooker and the Elizabethans thought of law as realizable pattern. The pattern's claim to realization was taken to be self-evident.

In the case of man this claim to realization of pattern is never taken for granted. The pattern can and ought to be realized. Man, however, is both free and froward. And for man's nature to realize itself at all normal development is required, proper growth and full exercise of reason before the pattern can materialize or be maintained. And in actual fact, among men, reason is both unequally distributed and of unequal growth.

The drawback of unequal distribution and unequal growth need not be fatal. It is here that Custom comes in. Custom is the expression of the inner pattern of Nature, the basis of Law, and the practical guide for man. During long periods of time and over large numbers of men the absolute shape will tend to establish itself, for the ideal arrangement is actually the most satisfactory: man works best when he works in accordance with his real nature. It is only this real nature, in fact, which gives him his proper fit in the community of things and people which constitutes his universe. There will always be, therefore, a tendency in man towards the ideal form. In the normal way he will adjust himself to that pattern which is actually the one—and the only one—in which he feels right. To see a near approximation to the pattern he need only look at the customs of his fathers.

Man can only know himself in terms of his proper place. Place here means his relation to the rest of his environment, human and non-human. It follows necessarily, therefore, that his main task is to conform. The individual pattern can only be preserved by a man maintaining his right position in regard to the grand universal pattern.

Thus, from two sides, the individual might draw a counsel of limitation and self-restraint. The Elizabethan is not infinite, as the Romantic is, through inherence in him of 'the Whole'. He is and must always be a finite intelligence. His intelligence, however, will be sufficient for him to recognize and perform his function. He is not 'the Whole', he is only a part of the whole pattern. But he is necessary, in his subordinate way, to the pattern's completeness. To discover his true nature the Romantic would look into his own bosom. There he would have the dark intimation of his connection with roots in the Kingdom of Hela. The Elizabethan, on the other hand, would best discover the pattern of his inner nature by looking out on the world of his fellows and forefathers. In that world he would see the habitual grooves that successions of similar men had worn, the outlines of the form of their inner nature. He would conclude that the individual must first understand his intrinsic limitation. Then, wisely, he must observe tradition. Restraint, therefore, as well as Reason and Benevolence, are inalienably associated with Nature. So far as man is reasonable he will also conform. The long-established can safely be presumed to approximate to the eternal. The opinion which is sufficiently widely held will be near enough the truth:

The general and perpetual voice of men is the sentence of God himself. For that which men have at all times learned, Nature herself must needs have taught; and God being the author of Nature, her voice is but his instrument. By her from him we receive whatsoever in such sort we learn. Infinite duties there are, the goodness whereof is by this rule sufficiently manifested, although we had no other warrant besides to approve them . . . by force of the light of Reason, wherewith God illuminateth everyone which cometh into the world, men being able to know truth from falsehood, and good from evil, do thereby learn in many things what the will of God is; which will himself not revealing by any extraordinary means unto them, but they by natural discourse attaining the knowledge thereof. . . . Axioms less general, yet so manifest that they require no further proof, are such as these, 'God to be worshipped'; 'parents to be honoured'; 'others to be used by us as we ourselves would be by them'. Such things, as soon as they are alleged, all men acknowledge to be good; they require no proof or further discourse to be assured of their goodness. (Bk. I, Ch. viii, 3–5.)

It will be noticed that the lines laid down by Custom, for Hooker, are by no means merely external ones. The contour he delineates is that of man's inward constitution. And the list of truths axiomatic for man is calmly and confidently given. It is a shocking amount of decency to ascribe to unaccommodated man.

Not everyone, even in Hooker's time, shared the same full calm and confidence. As we shall see, *King Lear* incorporates alternatives to this rational optimism, just as it incorporates the Thunder. Hooker's axiomatic decencies, however, are those which Lear himself holds to. It is these decencies he sees his daughters continually violating, and in expostulating with them he voices an essentially Anglican conscience.

When, for example, Goneril has forced Lear from her own castle, Lear turns hopefully to Regan. To the younger daughter he says:

> No, Regan, thou shalt never have my curse:
> Thy tender-hefted Nature shall not give
> Thee o'er to harshness: her eyes are fierce, but thine
> Do comfort, and not burn. 'Tis not in thee
> To grudge my pleasures, to cut off my train,
> To bandy hasty words, to scant my sizes,
> And in conclusion, to oppose the bolt
> Against my coming in. Thou better know'st
> The offices of Nature, bond of childhood,
> Effects of courtesy, dues of gratitude.   (II, ii.)

27

Lear's theology of Nature here is neither pagan nor Ancient British. We see the same benign system in the temperate sunshine of Hooker's prose or in the dapplings of Bacon's allegory. Lear's Nature, like theirs, is a structure ascending from primordial matter up to God. It, too, takes for granted that parents are to be honoured and human decencies observed. It assumes as the absolute shape for man an image of tenderness, comfort, generosity, charity, courtesy, gratitude.

One last great thing might be pointed to in the Elizabethan view of benignant Nature. It is this—Man's nature is not a minimum to which man can be reduced; it is not the skeleton Housman's Lad will give birth to in the grave; it is rather a maximum which man must attain, and this maximum will involve the successful and willing co-operation of man and his world before the richest image of man will be realized. Co-operation is essential if the pattern is to be fulfilled. Man will reach his right stature only under favouring conditions, by consent of his fellows and circumstance. Hostility from either will constitute 'impediment or let'. It is in this sense that Hooker expounds St. Paul, in a passage important for an understanding of Nature: our intention must be towards a maximum to be realized, rather than towards a minimal bare sufficiency beyond which the human cannot be reduced:

All men desire to lead in this world a happy life. That life is led most happily, wherein all virtue is exercised without impediment or let. The Apostle, in exhorting men to contentment although they have in the world no more than very bare food and raiment, giveth us thereby to understand that those are even the lowest things necessary; that if we should be stripped of all those things without which we might possibly be, yet these must be left; that destitution in these is such an impediment, as till it be removed suffereth not the mind of man to admit any other care. (Bk I, Ch. x, 2.)

Hooker is arguing that because we can do without is no reason why we should do without. Destitution, the bare minimum, is anti-human and unnatural. The ideal for man is not the beggar but the King. Though Nature involves self-control and self-limitation, it does not demand self-mutilation. It is large and free-handed. Nature is not a niggard. This, too, is stated emphatically in *King Lear*.

It is stated in two ways. Shakespeare's image of utter destitution is, of course, Poor Tom. King Lear confronts the Beggarman. Crazed now, the King sees the Beggar as the very essence of man, 'the thing itself . . . unaccommodated man . . . a poor, bare, fork'd animal'. Lear's encounter with Poor Tom is an incident in his madness. But before he is mad he has met with unnatural niggardliness in his daughters.

They have argued for retrenchment and reform on Lear's part. Lear must whittle down those things he thinks of as demanded by his position. Lear's exasperated reply to their argument is in complete accord with Hooker:

> O reason not the need: our basest beggars
> Are in the poorest things superfluous,
> Allow not Nature more than Nature needs:
> Man's life is cheap as beast's. Thou art a Lady;
> If only to go warm were gorgeous,
> Why Nature needs not what thou gorgeous wear'st,
> Which scarcely keeps thee warm, but for true need,
> You Heavens, give me that patience, patience I need.
>
> (II, ii.)

Lear does not take the ingratitude as an offence against himself. It is a violation of Nature. As if to assert his own adherence to the centre of the pattern that his daughters' conduct denies, he recalls himself abruptly and refuses to retaliate. He appeals to heaven for patience. Patience is of all things the most necessary to a man tried as he is. Patience is the 'precious pearl', prophylactic against the mortal sin of forsaking charity and falling into wrath. His judgment of his daughters' conduct, however, still holds good. They are reversing the procedure proper to 'natural theology'. They are bent on rushing down the scale. To turn one's back on man the accommodated creature, at his most glorious a King, is to turn one's back on God.

Lear's impetuous argument still has time to make an intellectual pun:

> If only to go warm were gorgeous,
> Why Nature needs not what thou gorgeous wear'st,
> Which scarcely keeps thee warm.

Lear is taking the argument begun by his daughters, here, and
reapplying it as a *tu quoque*. The first two lines follow the thought
of minimal human needs. 'Gorgeous' at first calls up the image
of overdress. Then, amazingly rapidly, this is replaced by the
image of undress. The lewd daughters are perverting clothes
from their proper use. Nature is thus doubly affronted by a
gorgeousness that mimics (and in royalty) the half-nakedness of
the Beggarman.

In condemning his daughters Lear is tacitly condemning the
unjust social order in which they stand. His remarks are a fore-
shadowing of the egalitarian prayer on the Heath. Nature rebuking them is also rebuking the perverted society for which
they are standards. (Incidentally, the Elizabethan Homilies are
constantly attacking the crime of 'gorgeousness' of raiment). In
one sense, the sisters are of course very properly dressed: they
might be, indeed, models of fashionable show. At the same time
not all customs are good. While good custom is to be revered as
the expression of men's common nature, perverse and unnatural custom can at all times creep in and become established.
The theory of Nature did not necessarily commit one to the
status quo no matter what. The standards to be observed are not
derived from society. Society in fact must conform to what the
reasonable man, by God's light, would recognize as natural.
Hooker himself makes the point:

I deny not but lewd and wicked custom, beginning perhaps at the
first among few, afterwards spreading into greater multitudes, and so
continuing from time to time, may be of force even in plain things to
smother the light of natural understanding. (Bk. I, Ch. viii, 11.)

Not all established patterns are necessarily the absolute shape.

It is possible for customs to be unnatural and for societies to be corrupt. Hooker makes the point, and it is implicit, too, I think, in what Lear says. Subsequently he will take up other positions from which to arraign society. Here his criticism follows from the stand he takes in orthodox Nature.

[III]

THE MALIGNANT NATURE OF HOBBES, EDMUND, AND THE WICKED DAUGHTERS

Lear's criticism of corrupt custom from his stand in the ground of Nature is a convenient point at which to leave the benevolent and orthodox Nature and look at that Nature in the play which opposes it. Edmund, too, insists that customs can be unreasonable, and societies unnatural. In contrast to Lear and Hooker, he finds it quite easy to 'treat of metaphysics or of the internal and immutable in nature without rushing at once into natural theology'. Or rather, his natural theology is in ironical opposition to Lear's. Edmund worships a Goddess of whom neither Hooker nor Bacon would approve:

> Thou Nature art my Goddess, to thy Law
> My services are bound, wherefore should I
> Stand in the plague of custom, and permit
> The curiosity of Nations to deprive me?
> For that I am some twelve, or fourteene Moonshines
> Lag of a Brother? Why Bastard? Wherefore base?
> When my dimensions are as well compact,
> My mind as generous, and my shape as true
> As honest Madam's issue? Why brand they us
> With Base? With baseness Bastardie? Base, Base?
> Who in the lusty stealth of Nature, take
> More composition and fierce quality,
> Than doth within a dull stale tired bed
> Goe to th' creating a whole tribe of Fops
> Got 'tween a sleep, and wake? Well then,

> Legitimate Edgar, I must have your land;
> Our Father's love, is to the Bastard Edmund,
> As to th' legitimate: fine word: Legitimate.
> Well, my Legitimate, if this letter speed,
> And my invention thrive, Edmund the base
> Shall to th' Legitimate: I grow, I prosper:
> Now Gods, stand up for Bastards.   (I, ii.)

No medieval devil ever bounced on to the stage with a more scandalous self-announcement.

The sentiments of Edmund's speech must have been fairly widespread in Shakespeare's society. There is no doubt that similar ethical views were implicit in the eminent generality of public conduct at any time during the sixteenth and seventeenth centuries. It was not, however, an acceptable view. Giordano Bruno's death was ascribable to a meaning for 'Nature' no more revolutionary than this. To a post-Darwinian age, of course, the Nature Edmund addresses as Goddess is a deceptively familiar commonplace. We follow Edmund easily when he appeals from Custom. We understand him when he prefers to regard it as a system of merely local and arbitrary peculiarities. We sympathize when he points to the urgent personal drives it is obstructing, when he calls attention to his handsome body, his superior intelligence, the vigorous animality derived from 'the lusty stealth of Nature'. Each of his arguments awakens answering echoes in a modern mind. Whatever Goddess this is, she seems the guardian of powers we approve: strength of mind, animal vigour, handsome appearance, instinctive appetite, impatience with humbug, iconoclastic force. Edmund might be Peer Gynt.

It would be possible, also, for Bacon and Hooker to include Edmund in their scheme. The figure of Pan, in Bacon's allegory, is half animal and half human. Bacon explains the nicety of this as follows:

> Again, the body of nature is justly described bi-form, because of the difference between its superior and inferior parts [*i.e. between the*

sphere of incorruption above the moon, and of corruption below it].
This bi-form figure also represents the participation of one species with
another, for there appear to be no simple natures, but all participate or
consist of two: thus man has somewhat of the brute, the brute somewhat of the plant, the plant somewhat of the mineral: so that all natural
bodies have really two faces, or consist of a superior and an inferior
species.

Every natural body has two faces because each creature is inter-
mediary between a higher and a lower. Intrinsically each thing
is compound. We can define its constitution (its 'nature') as
soon as we have defined its position. But the grand Nature is
not only a series of positions, an order neutral in respect of its
general arrangement. The whole system has orientation, too.
Supervening on the local nature which derives from position,
there is disposition (in our modern and derivative sense). It is
axiomatic that one should look to the higher. Nature has a
nisus towards the topmost point of the pyramid—the point at
which we rush into natural theology.

This *nisus* is not what men invariably do have. It is what they
inevitably should have. One's nature will be lost in default of not
having it: one will slide from one's position. One's nature, however, is not a structure laid down. It is an absolute shape to be
realized. It requires for this realization, reason to see, and will to
persist in the co-operation with God's pattern.

But ever since the first lapse, man's reason has been clouded
and his will enfeebled: 'The minds of men', Hooker says, 'being
so darkened as they are with the foggy damp or original corruption'; 'and the laws of nature', as Bacon would add, created
perfect by God in the first days, having 'received a revocation, in
part, by the curse'. Man originally made a wrong choice and man
subsequently has been constantly rebelling. Edmund could be
explained as such a rebel, preferring the inferior parts to the
superior.

The view that each creature is compound of two 'natures'
does not necessarily involve a dualistic view either of the creature

C   33

concerned or of the universe in which it participates. It obviously lends itself, however, to dualism. The two parts of man which when properly related form the unity of absolute shape can be regarded as hostile contestants representing irreconcilable powers. Such a view was widely current in Elizabethan times. The Stoics, of course, had originally opposed Reason to the Passions. The picture of Pan, and a view of man as half good and half bad, was perpetuated in the Mermaid of the Bestiaries. What we conceive as orientation was more easily picturable in the sixteenth century as a rivalry between competitors. Picturesque value, for example, determines Launcelot Andrewes' use of the Manichaean view to illustrate a point in his sermon on Genesis, I, 1:

> The good and white God made the Heaven, and Man from the middle upward: And the black and evill God was the efficient cause of the Earth, and of Man from the middle downward.

Lear has this Manichaean vision of women when he falls from reason into madness:

> Down from the waist they are Centaurs, though women all above: but to the girdle do the gods inherit, beneath is all the Fiends. (IV, vi.)

Edmund could be the votary of the black and evil god.

Shakespeare, however, does not make Edmund a diabolist. As we shall see in the succeeding chapter Edmund is the last of a line of villains that begins with Richard III. Richard was consciously diabolical. He was aware of the challenge he threw to the supernatural. His 'Have mercy Jesu!' at the end of the play indicates the recognition that his defeat comes from God. Edmund is not like Richard in this respect. His soliloquy is not a challenge to a higher law. It is the manifesto of a superior enlightenment to dimmer-witted gulls. It has all the passionate warmth and cool aplomb of common sense rampant. It is amused, too, because it is contemptuous of the prospective victims who cannot overhear it. Edmund is not a devil. He is, on the contrary, a normal, sensible, reasonable fellow: but emancipated. His knowledge of what Nature is like is a real knowledge of what she really is like.

There was a current doubt in Shakespeare's time as to what Nature really was like. The doubt pervades the whole of *King Lear* and gives each positive affirmation in the play its peculiar tenseness and clarity. The main ambiguity finds expression whenever Thunder comes into the play. But this we shall return to later. Meantime the dilemma can best be illustrated from the *Faerie Queene*, in a passage which gets us closer to the terms of Edmund's speech than anything of Hooker's or Bacon's:

> Then forth issewed (great goddesse) great dame Nature
> With goodly port and gracious Majesty,
> Being far greater and more tall of stature
> Then any of the gods or Powers on hie:
> Yet certes by her face and physnomy,
> Whether she man or woman inly were,
> That could not any creature well descry;
> For with a veile, that wimpled everywhere,
> Her head and face was hid that mote to none appeare.
>
> That, some do say, was so by skill devized
> To hide the terror of her uncouth hew
> From mortall eyes that should be sore aggrized;
> For that her face did like a Lion shew,
> That eye of wight could not indure to view;
> But others tell that it so beautious was,
> And round about such beames of splendor threw,
> That it the Sunne a thousand times did pass,
> Ne could be seene but like an image in a glass.
>   (Bk. VII, viii, 5-6.)

The orthodox view keeps the ideas of Nature and God in the most intimate association. There was a tendency running counter to this in Renaissance thought, a tendency to separate the two. Fuller's Atheist, for example, is a man who will not see 'the arms of the God of Heaven' in every creature in the world, 'even from worms to men,' but ascribes everything 'either to chance . . . or else to nature, which is a mere sleight of the devil to conceal God from men by calling him after another name'. The idea of nature as a self-running machine, set going by an absentee deity, capable of being measured and investigated—the nature, in other words, of science—was beginning to establish itself. From this 'Nature' the realizable normative world of 'absolute shapes'—that which is constitutive of man's reason, is part of God's nature, and decides that supervening orientation which makes of orderly arrangement an ethical programme too —this world which makes order dynamic was omitted. Nature becomes given structure instead of normative pattern.

We see the change in this way because of a subsequent clarification of the problem in the developed scientific Nature of Descartes and Newton. Spenser, however, saw the alternatives as a goddess who might really wear a Lion's head or a woman's. The woman-headed goddess is the Nature of Hooker. It is a Nature of such absolute shape as can only be viewed in a mirror. But if the other alternative is true and the Goddess is Lion-headed (a grim inversion of the Bestiary Mermaid and of Bacon's Pan) it means that Nature excludes the values called human, and the norms called Reason: 'God to be worshipped', 'parents to be honoured' 'others to be used by us as we ourselves would be by them'. Spenser leaves the reader with a doubt, or presents him with a choice. The Goddess's portrait might be typical eclecticism, vagueness, or indifference. It is maybe better to regard it as part of the sage Spenserian seriousness: Spenser chooses to leave the choice with us.

Edmund is in no doubt as to which choice he makes. His Goddess is Lion-headed. Man is merely the King of the beasts. Though he can arraign society equally with Lear, he does it from an opposite quarter. He has inverted the scale that 'rushes into natural theology'. He deifies 'the inferior parts'.

A change in the meaning of Reason accompanies the change in the meaning of Nature. The dualism of Reason *versus* the Passions is useless to explain Edmund. Though Edmund is

Appetite, he is also a rationalist. It is only that Reason for him
is something different from the Reason of Lear or Gloster.
Reason, of course, is another concept the orthodox never separated from God and Nature. In the contrasted views of Edmund
and Gloster concerning our relations to 'the Stars' the two
Reasons voice themselves:

GLOSTER: These late eclipses in the sun and moon portend no good to
us: though the wisdom of Nature can reason it thus, and thus, yet
Nature finds itself scourg'd by the sequent effects, Love cools,
friendship falls off, brothers divide. In cities, mutinies; in countries,
discord; in palaces, treason; and the bond crack'd, 'twixt son and
father. This villain of mine comes under the prediction; there's son
against father; the King falls from bias of Nature, there's father
against child. We have seen the best of our time....

Exit.

EDMUND: This is the excellent foppery of the world, that when we are
sick in fortune, often the surfeits of our own behaviour, we make
guilty of our disasters, the sun, the moon, and stars, as if we were
villains on necessity, fools by heavenly compulsion, knaves, thieves,
and treachers by spherical predominance. Drunkards, liars, and
adulterers by an inforc'd obedience of planetary influence; and all
that we are evil in, by a divine thrusting on. An admirable evasion
of whoremaster man, to lay his goatish disposition on the charge of
a star. My father compounded with my mother under the Dragon's
tail, and my nativity was under *Ursa Major*, so that it follows, I am
rough and lecherous. I should have been that I am, had the maidenliest star in the firmament twinkled on my bastardizing.' (I, ii.)

Belief or disbelief in astrology was not in the sixteenth century
definitive of orthodoxy. Bishop Coverdale considered astro-
logical influence a reasonable likelihood. Roger Hutchinson, the
Puritan divine and mid-sixteenth century headmaster of Eton,
on the other hand, dismissed it as little better than heathenism.
Spenser, in *A View of the Present State of Ireland*, thought with
the Bastard that 'it is the manner of men, that when they are
fallen into any absurditye, or theyr actions succeede not as they
would, they are ready allwayes to impute the blame thereof
unto the heavens, soe to excuse their owne follyes and imperfec-

tiones'. The important thing is the relation conceived as existing between Man and Nature. What Reason is will turn on what these two are thought to be.

Gloster's 'wisdom of Nature' I take to mean 'the scientific account of natural happenings': the sort of explanation Cicero gives in *Julius Caesar* of the miracle-charged thunder-storm over Rome the night Caesar is murdered. Gloster clings for his own part, however, to a view which sees physical nature as more than a realm of indifferent law. The eclipses are not efficient causes in a closed natural sphere of efficient causes: that is how Edmund regards them. They are not even efficient causes of the catastrophes that seem to accompany them. They are symptoms of a disease which affects all nature. And the disease is bound to break out in man's world too.

Edmund, on the other hand, admits of no connections in Nature save connections of material cause and effect. And Nature is a closed system. For him, as for us, it is a structure laid down, devoid of intelligence, impervious to Reason. This being so it is ridiculous to blame the stars for one's misfortunes. Nature is dead mechanism, and it does not include man, except as he is an animal body. Apart from his body, man has a mind. As mind, man is free of nature and superior to it. He knows its laws, he can manipulate it for a given effect. Human nature, too, can be known and manipulated. The machiavel will know it better than anyone else, and he will be freer to manipulate it. It is significant that in the figure of Edmund the sense of separation from nature and superiority to it goes with a sense of the individual's separation from the community and a feeling of superiority to his fellows. As Nature goes dead, community becomes competition, and man a nexus of appetites. Reason is no longer a normative drive but a calculator of the means to satisfy the appetites with which we were born.

Edmund's philosopher, we have said, is Hobbes—born in the Armada year and surviving to philosophise into the Restoration. Hobbes's vision of man in society is the projection on to a philo-

sophic plane of Edmund, Goneril, and Regan. These three constitute for Hobbes the essential model of humanity.

Hobbes begins with appetite, 'the universal wolf':

> ... the felicity of this life consisteth not in the repose of a mind satis-
> fied. For there is no such *finis ultimus*, utmost aim, nor *summum bonum*,
> greatest good, as is spoken of in the books of the old moral philoso-
> phers. Nor can a man any more live, whose desires are at an end, than
> he whose senses and imaginations are at a stand. Felicity is a continual
> progress of the desire, from one object to another, the attaining of the
> former being still but the way to the latter.... So that in the first place,
> I put for a general inclination of all mankind, a perpetual and restless
> desire of power after power, that ceaseth only in death. (*Leviathan*,
> Ch. XI.)

Along with this restless megalomania goes paranoia: 'the passion
to be reckoned upon is fear'. The two together make for a bad
infinity of competition and mutual suspicion:

> ... therefore if any two men desire the same thing, which neverthe-
> less they cannot both enjoy, they become enemies; and in the way to
> their end, which is principally their own conservation, and sometimes
> their delectation only, endeavour to destroy or subdue one another.
> (*Leviathan*, Ch. XIII.)

Men take no natural delight in society unless overawed by a
Prince: 'men have no pleasure, but on the contrary a great deal
of griefe, in keeping company'....

> ... so that in the nature of man, we find three principal causes of
> quarrel. First, competition; secondly, diffidence; thirdly, glory. The
> first maketh men invade for gain; the second for safety; and the third,
> for reputation.... Hereby it is manifest that during the time men live
> without a common power to keep them all in awe, they are in that
> condition which is called war; and such a war, as is of every man,
> against every man ... continual fear and danger of violent death; and
> the life of man, solitary, poor, nasty, brutish, and short. (*Leviathan*,
> Ch. XIII.)

As we read the pages of dry and conscientious observation

other voices than Edmund's come to supply an undertone of comment:

GONERIL: This man hath had good counsel, a hundred knights?
　　　　'Tis politic, and safe to let him keep
　　　　At point a hundred knights: yes, that on every dream,
　　　　Each buzz, each fancy, each complaint, dislike,
　　　　He may enguard his dotage with their powers,
　　　　And hold our lives in mercy. . . .
ALBANY: Well, you may fear too far.
GONERIL: Safer than trust too far;
　　　　Let me still take away the harms I fear,
　　　　Not fear still to be taken.　　　　　　　　　　(I, iv.)

It might be noted in passing that here again (it is obvious in Edmund's first soliloquy) characters are shown taking decisions. And the field of choice is tense with important alternatives. *King Lear* makes more use of deliberate choice as a means of characterization than any other of Shakespeare's plays with the possible exception of *Antony and Cleopatra*. The effect of this on characterization is immediate. None of the characters are complex, yet each has an unmistakeable richness of significance and an emphatic vitality. The richness and vitality come from the way in which they are related, through decision, to the abruptly contoured Nature which forms the general background. The richness is a matter of the profound or horrifying overtones which the context of Nature provides. The characters thus call for the same kind of treatment as the characters of Morality. They are not Morality-figures. They stand one stage nearer to actuality than the personages of allegory. The clear Morality outline is however included in the play. The unambiguous Morality statement is presented in the deliberate stance each character adopts in the clearly-marked field. Thus Albany in this passage is obviously the voice of Nature in the benevolent sense of Hooker. Goneril is expressing Hobbes's alternative. What each says is 'common sense'. It is only through their vivid juxtaposition here that we are made to realize how far common sense itself is merely the afterbirth of decisions, acts of choice already made. Common sense will take one down the dip-slope, the other down the scarp-slope from this divide. Two persons are contrasted, but also two natures, two destinies for man. Throughout the play we are constantly prevented from taking a local view of the situation developing. The play presents the fate of man, the situation of man, in general.

The key-word in Goneril's speech is 'politic'. By it Shakespeare reminds his audience of the race of machiavels he has been dealing with since *Henry VI*. He points also to a constant challenge to a whole range of meanings which his generation felt to be a serious one. Goneril's other word is 'dotage'. By this her common sense forces us to examine the presuppositions of any common sense we would, with Albany, oppose to hers. By it she forces us out of the comfortable static positions of common sense. We are made to review the acts of choice our common sense depends on—and their implications.

The 'three principal causes of quarrel' in human nature Hobbes found to be 'competition, diffidence, glory': the impulse to acquire, to provide for one's security, to extend one's prestige. Edmund and the two sisters are made to a recipe equally simple. All that needs to be added to Hobbes in order to account for them is lust. We have described their characters as soon as we have itemized these ingredients. One detail in the picture of the sisters, however, might be pointed to. Bradley does not overlook it, but does not, I think, sufficiently stress it. It is an indication of Shakespeare's conscious concern with the abstract theme in the play. The information has little dramatic relevance at the point where it occurs. Its whole force comes from the way in which it links up with the play's intellectual content.—Before Edmund meets them, and before the rejection of Lear has been contemplated, war between the sisters is already rumoured as imminent. It is as if Shakespeare were underlining the Hobbesian account of human nature, its inherent competitiveness based on fear, its mechanical 'every man against every man'. The Hobbesian conception needs for its embodiment at least *two* daughters. As characters these will have to be practically indistinguishable: they will be at odds because of their alikeness. Allegory need go no further.

War, of course, does not break out as expected. The sisters unite against their father and the more urgent threat from France. Edmund's appearance, however, provides a further occasion for the exercise of their nature. All the sisters' appetites are activated. They plot each other's death, and that of their husbands, in rivalry for the exclusive right to Edmund's person. Edmund himself, meanwhile, is content to use their desires to further his own designs.

To sum up, Edmund and the sisters can be regarded as figures in a Morality debate concerning the nature of Man. They stand for the view given expression later by Hobbes. They are opposed to the view maintained in Hooker and Bacon. In Edmund's soliloquy we saw the reflection of a new rationality opposed to the old-fashioned Reason of Lear. Goneril and Albany's argument similarly puts one common sense against a common sense that has nothing in common with it. The Reason of Edmund and the common sense of Goneril belong to a view with which a modern audience, after Darwin, can readily sympathize. (A modern book, for example, has been written to show that the sisters are more sinned against than sinning.) Edmund and the Sisters, in spite of that, are the villains of the play.

They are not, however, monsters. There is no suggestion of melodrama in the portraiture. On the contrary, Shakespeare is at pains to make them eminently normal people. They are normal in the sense that they behave as we unfortunately expect people to behave. They are normal also in that the kind of behaviour they exhibit was coming to be regarded as standard behaviour (Hobbes adopts the standard). Shakespeare in fact even goes further than this. Goneril and Regan are not only eminently normal. They are also eminently respectable. They are the unco' guid in the play. They stand precisely for what Hal stands for when he turns away Falstaff.

[IV]

THE TWO NATURES AND THE FISSION OF ELIZABETHAN SOCIETY

The two parties in the play have two Natures and two Reasons. Common sense means a different thing for each because it rests on contrary acts of choice.

The orthodox always kept the ideas Reason, Nature, God and Man (as King) close together. In this context Reason is a real common sense. It implies a content on which all men agree. To us this content might appear nothing more than a number of laudable aims. For Hooker and the Elizabethans generally, on the other hand, there was no doubt about the real status of that which Reason descried and which gave Reason its definite body of axioms. Our norms were for them forms, and the forms 'some absolute shape or mirror'. This Reason was constitutive of man, part of the immanence of God in his creature. The same Reason was constitutive also of physical Nature: each thing in its degree, keeping station, being what it was because of where it was, yet having disposition as well as position—and that disposition a kind of innocent observance of Law: the whole system manifesting the virtues of co-operation, regularity, harmony.

Orthodox man felt himself to be part of the grand system of Nature in a real sense. Both his body and his mind were included. His attitude to Nature could not therefore be that of the observant analyst or the industrious watchmaker. Reason did not mean knowledge of how a thing is put together, or of how a thing works. Reason's primary work was to guide man in the exercise of his own nature: it illuminated the path man alone,

43

of all the creatures, had to follow. Secondly, it was that which could recognize in the grand external order the aesthetic and moral virtues important also in man's own sphere. Reason could not pierce the envelope of the other of Nature's creatures, nor did it need to. Their inner constitution—as far as Reason could descry one—was given in their observable position. Questions of constitution apart from status could not be raised. Creaturely wisdom could not in any case span the wisdom of the Creator. Thus what we should refer to the investigator for further research ('Let them anatomize Regan, see what breeds about her heart') the Elizabethan would refer to Reason and 'rush into natural theology'. From his position in the grand system Man drew his portion of natural stuff, half animal, half angelic. His task then was to exercise his function, to realize the absolute pattern, to obey the normative urges and controls he and all men were born to develop.

The attitude was unscientific only because wisdom was put before understanding. Scientific knowledge, it could be urged, was in any case limited: it could never circumscribe the infinite. Furthermore, in whatever quantities it might be accumulated, it would not be the kind of knowledge appropriate for man's moral illumination. Instead of pursuing, therefore, the interminable and inappropriate, man should cultivate the definite and particularly human, the proper goods of Reason. This he both can do and should do, and so preserve the absolute shape, generally agreed upon, morally approvable, aesthetically right —his own, yet Nature's too, and God's.

Edmund in his opening soliloquy is the compact image of everything that denies the orthodox view. Shakespeare thought of him simply and inclusively as the Bastard, and 'bastard' is the Elizabethan equivalent of 'outsider'. Edmund is a complete Outsider. He is outside Society, he is outside Nature, he is outside Reason. Man, Nature, and God now fall apart. Reason, for Hooker the principle of coherence for all three, dwindles to something regulative rather than constitutive. It is an analyser, a cold calculator. Its knowledge is the knowledge of the watch-maker or engineer, an understanding of cogs and springs and levers, of mining and counter-mining. Nature itself becomes a machine this Reason can have this knowledge of. Descartes' dualism is implicit in Edmund's reasoning on the stars. The New Man is a Mind and a Body. The body belongs to mechanical Lion-headed Nature. The mind stands outside as observer and server of the machine.

Nature is inert and dead. The *nisus* in things has disappeared. Now a thing's nature is laid down in its constitution—a stuff of matter and a propellant of appetite. We cannot change our nature or the nature of others. We can only express our nature, and others' natures we can use: for our own advantage. We can make them our tools by a superior knowledge of how they work. That science is an endless pursuit is no objection. The important thing is the marginal advantage to be gained by having a sharper wit than one's rival in the same field. Edmund curiously and confidently says:

'I would be that I am had the maidenliest star in the firmament twinkled on my bastardizing.'

He is not a co-operative member of a grand community. He means that his nature is given and unalterable and separate and his own. Nothing supervenes on the isolation of each individual position. Disposition—the idea of orientation in Nature and Man—has disappeared.

The dualism of mind and body means that the body supplies the needs—a *vis a tergo*—and mind supplies the ways and means to satisfy them. The dualism applied to society means that the jarring of original atoms has been lifted to the human level. Every man is against every man. In place of the King the new symbol is the 'politician': the man who can play on human nature (the machine of *Leviathan*) better than any other. The mechanical manipulation of human nature was maybe prior to the mechanical manipulation of physical nature. It was maybe the politician who gave the scientist his cue. In Edmund, at any rate, politic machiavel and renaissance scientist—two vast images—are fused. In addition Edmund is the careerist on the make, the New Man laying a mine under the crumbling walls and patterned streets of an ageing society that thinks it can disregard him.

For the two Natures and two Reasons imply two societies. Edmund belongs to the new age of scientific inquiry and industrial development, of bureaucratic organization and social regimentation, the age of mining and merchant-venturing, of monopoly and Empire-making, the age of the sixteenth century and after: an age of competition, suspicion, glory. He hypostatizes those trends in man which guarantee success under the new conditions—one reason why his soliloquy is so full of what we recognize as common sense. These trends he calls Nature. And with this Nature he identifies Man. Edmund would not agree that any other Nature was thinkable.

Another Nature was being asserted, however, in Edmund's time, because there was another society not yet outgrown. This is the society of the sixteenth century and before. The standards Edmund rejects have come down from the Middle Ages. They assume a co-operative, reasonable decency in man, and respect for the whole as being greater than the part: 'God to be worshipped, parents to be honoured, others to be used by us as we ourselves would be by them.' The medieval procedure was to mutualize conflicting claims by agreeing over limits. Edmund's instinct is to recognize no limits save those coming from incapacity to get one's way.

Edmund's main significance consists in this. He is not part of a playwright's dream. He is a direct imaging of the times. If we see him in the Shakespearian context of the Natures we can regard him as a symbol. If we think in terms of the historical setting Shakespeare himself belonged to, he is an actuality.

We have maintained that Hobbes is Edmund's philosopher. Hobbes's world of the 1640's is only different from the world of the 1600's in being a slightly more developed form of the same thing. The matter presented in *Leviathan* Jacobean drama, as a vital organ of thought, had already pondered. It is matter, too, that history had been enacting any time after 1500. Hobbes took over Edmund and made him his basic pattern. The version of humanity thus supplied provided, as Hobbes thought, a ready-made argument for absolute monarchy. There can be no society for Yahoos except an order imposed from above. Unfortunately, as a philosopher only, Hobbes lacked the army he would have needed to impose his views. He had to rely on an appeal to reason. And for men to adopt his system they should have to possess the sort of 'reason' he denied to exist: Hooker's Reason. Friends pointed out to Hobbes the fallacy of his position. He must have been aware himself of his own futility. The obstacles to the adoption of his views he analyses accurately and concisely, and in so doing gives a good picture of the working group-interests of his world:

But they say again, that though [my] principles be right, yet common people are not of capacity enough to be made to understand them. I should be glad that the rich and potent subjects of a Kingdom, or those that are accounted the most learned, were no less incapable than they. But all men know that the obstructions to [my] kind of doctrine proceed, not so much from the difficulty of the matter, as from the interest of them that are to learn. Potent men digest hardly anything that setteth up a power to bridle their affections; and learned men anything that discovereth their errors, and thereby lesseneth their authority: whereas the common people's minds, unless they be tainted with dependence on the potent, or scribbled over with the opinions of their doctors, are like clean paper. (*Leviathan*, Ch. XXX.)

Hobbes catalogues among 'those things that weaken or tend to the dissolution of a commonwealth', monopolies ('a disease which resembleth the pleurisy'), potent subjects with a popular following, Enthusiasm (or private judgment), and Great Towns. The subject matter of his philosophy was contemporary man in contemporary society. Even more than Bacon Hobbes is abreast of the times. The interest of his account for us is the application it is possible to make to the 1600's—yet another link between Edmund and the philosopher. Essex is an instance of what Hobbes saw as the first threat to his commonwealth: a potent man, who held monopolies, had a popular following, and led a mutiny in the city of London. Shakespeare could observe for himself the kind of world Hobbes is writing about.

Just as Shakespeare could witness in his own environment the clash between the old economy and the new business methods, so in his own biography he knew what it was to be in transit between two worlds. The son of a small farmer-leather-merchant-butcher-glovemaker who lost both money and status in his country town, he had come up to London to snatch at opportunity, as the Bastard in *King John* or Edmund in *King Lear* had arrived at Court to carve for themselves. In London he lived on the best of both and all the worlds. He had a rich patron on one side and a share in the going Burbage concern on the other; the artist's temperament was combined with the business man's good sense; the approval of court wit offset the applause of popular audience; and when he had made enough money in business to set up as a country gentleman, he retired.

Edmund is the New Man. Shakespeare's understanding of the type is so extensive as to amount to real sympathy. The insight comes, I think, from Shakespeare's being in part a New Man himself. This would account for the colour and charm with which he always invests the figure. Be that as it may, Shakespeare has had ample time to observe that which he embodies in Edmund. Edmund is not a theory of human nature only, though his existence demands one. He is a fact. To inquire into the meaning he gives to 'Nature' is not merely to hunt for a new dictionary meaning. Nor in handling the old and the new meanings is Shakespeare writing an academic thesis. The ideas are people. The meanings are moving bits of a changing world.

An example paralleling Edmund's is the word 'Nature' in Lear's speech already quoted:

Then let them anatomize Regan; see what breeds about her heart.

Is there any cause in Nature that makes these hard hearts?

'Nature' here is pushed across an important threshold. The physical nature of science (the Nature Bacon mostly confines himself to in *Novum Organum*) is made to encroach on the territory of moral corruption. For strict orthodoxy the Fall of Man rather than anatomy should have been brought into the explanation. That is one thing the lines mean. For the other thing they mean we must look not into what men were thinking in Shakespeare's time but at what they were doing. We have to remember the negotiating of the Grand Lease, whereby, under pressure, the Prince Bishop of Durham gave over his palatinate coal mines to the Leicester group: particularly to Thomas Sutton, Jonson's Volpone. This is a spectacular encroachment of the secular entrepreneur on to territory that had been ecclesiastical time out of mind. Behind the shift and drift of the meanings of the word 'Nature' there is the shift and drift of humanity in a setting at once historical and spiritual. Behind the word there is Shakespeare certainly. But behind Shakespeare there is the mining engineer breaking into the bowels of the earth; the seeker out of the mysteries of brass, and glass, and salt, and the supplier of the Elizabethan navies; the doctor taking apart the human body to anatomize the mechanism of muscle and bone; the capitalist aware of money as the sinews of war and soon to recognize in it the circulating life-blood of the body politic. All these, too, are vitally concerned to alter the meaning of Nature: to extend the Nature which can be worked, made a tool of, got to produce profits; to minimize the theology which would contend for an aesthetic and moral attitude only to Nature, and which would find no argument in Nature for profit-making.

There is tremendous gusto in the portrait of the Bastard: energy, emancipation, a right-minded scorn of humbug, clear-headedness; the speed, sureness, and lissom courage of a tiger.

Edmund is the last great expression in Shakespeare of that side of Renaissance individualism which has made a positive addition to the heritage of the West. After *King Lear* the figure does not appear again. This is because, I think, in *King Lear* Shakespeare gives a final and exhaustive statement to the issues he has been handling throughout his chronicles since *Henry VI*. But in spite of the attractiveness of the portrait, Edmund still belongs with Goneril and Regan. He is a Shakespearian villain. And condemned with him in the apocalyptical judgment of the play is the corrupt society he represents.

It is part of Shakespeare's staggering inclusiveness of mind that he should endow the symbol with so much force and life at the same time as he recognizes the sinister implications of Edmund's attitude, if it should prevail:

> If that the heavens do not their visible spirits
> Send quickly down to tame this vile offence,
> It will come,
> Humanity must perforce prey on itself
> Like monsters of the deep.

(IV, ii.)

Though Edmund and the sisters are normal, they are only so in a special sense. They are perfect types of the human nature to which society (Shakespeare's and ours) gives survival value. Normality does not mean that they are not diseased. It is possible that the perfect adjustment might be to an imperfect, in fact to a corrupt, society.

Edmund is the antithesis to the benevolent thesis Shakespeare's age inherited from the Middle Ages. He embodies something vital which a final synthesis must reaffirm. But he makes an absolute claim which Shakespeare will not support. It is right for man to feel, as Edmund does, that society exists for man, not man for society. It is not right to assert the kind of man Edmund would erect to this supremacy. It is right that a man should find the perfect adjustment to his society that Edmund does, being as completely a part of history as Edmund is. It is wrong, how_ ever, unless the society is something radically different from that which Edmund espouses.

But it is no remedy to turn back the clock. Shakespeare's doubt over the traditional version of man's nature and society— a doubt dramatized in the person of the doting King who loses his wits—was largely due to an awareness of the essential injustice it involved, both for Edmund and Poor Tom. The danger of rational optimism as expressed in the traditional theology was that it could end by claiming that whatever is is right. As Edmund parodied it, it ascribed all we are evil in to a divine thrusting on. Absolute obedience was enjoined on the individual to both his temporal and his spiritual overlord. This obedience was urged in the name of an ideal order, compact of Reason and Nature. The Middle Ages supplied feasible grounds for such an obedience. The absolute principle was in fact vested in institutions. Society by intention aimed at equity and the realization of the absolute shape. Heresy consisted in denying the Spirit rather than the letter of the law. Ideally, the social configurations were not themselves absolute.

Professor Owst has argued strongly for the Preaching Friar as society's main critic, chastising any tendency to take advantage of the letter rather than submit to the spirit. Under the conditions of Tudor Despotism the medieval world-view became, however, less credible. Heresy now consists in challenging the letter of social order in the name of any spirit whatsoever. Authority is vested in a person. Elizabeth is absolute in the realms of both Pope and Emperor. She claims, in addition, to be the Virgin Queen. According to her Homilies rebellion is always and absolutely wrong, 'the whole puddle and sink of all sins against God and man'. By the sixteenth century the argument for unconditional obedience becomes more and more an ideology and less and less a way for the spirit. It is political propaganda in moralistic disguise. The duties imposed are the will of the Prince not the will of God. Under the Tudors the discrepancy between ideal programme and actual performance—apparent even to the Friars in the Middle Ages—is more obvious than ever. Even Hooker capitulates to the view of man-in-society as a Yahoo that needs the yoke:

Laws politic, ordained for external order and regimen amongst men, are never framed as they should be . . . unless presuming man to be in regard to his depraved mind little better than a wild beast.

This is the Fool's wiseman turning unexpectedly knave when he considers the justification of the authoritarian state. Society was supposed to be an ideal order—Troilus' Cressida. The same system in actuality could behave like Diomed's bitch. Troilus's dilemma when he sees his ideal in the arms of Diomed is Shakespeare's dilemma when he sees Nature claimed for the Virgin Queen and James (by Divine Right) the First.

Thus two societies must be added to the two Natures and two Reasons. Because the play is an allegory of ethical systems and people, it must also be an allegory of community. For according to one of the systems at least we are all members one of another. This society is that of the medieval vision. Its representative is an old King ('Nature in you stands on the very verge of her confine'). It is doting and it falls into error. The other society is that of nascent capitalism. Its representative in chief is the New Man—and a politic machiavel. I have no doubt that if Shakespeare were forced to take sides, he would prefer Lear to Goneril and Regan, Gloster to Edmund. Shakespeare, however, has an alternative to this simple either-or.

The Middle Ages dreamed of the *Civitas Dei*. Here the good man had a ground whereon to base himself, affirming faith in community while standing critically aside from the corrupt society. The sixteenth century, too, had its vision. The orthodox establishment was threatened from one side by the bogey of machiavellism, shaken from the other by the rumour of Anabaptism. Along with most sixteenth century theology the *Ecclesiastical Polity* controverts the views of Munzer as fervently as those of Rome and Geneva. Anabaptism was kept in mind, like Machiavel's doctrine, by the series of counterblasts against it. (The burnings of Baptists in Elizabeth's reign amounted to about a dozen only. The Baptist community—mainly of Dutch émigrés—was never more than about a hundred until James's reign.) By a profound instinct for the Utopian root of art, Shakespeare saw in the medieval dream and the Anabaptist equalitarianism an alternative to Edmund and a fulfilment of the old King's real Nature. The vision of the new order is given in Lear's prayer and embodied in the King's rejected daughter.

The outline of the allegory still continues clear.—The society with Nature and Reason as its aim can never be utterly lost. At its best, it still admits the constant need for approximation to the absolute pattern. The spirit is not denied for the sake of the letter. Such a society can grow old and dote and commit offence. But it never utterly rejects the possibility of, and therefore it is always open to, regeneration. The Old King in Shakespeare's play is actually launched on a course of regeneration after error and the nemesis of error. The saving fact is that he has a daughter

> Who redeems Nature from the general curse
> Which twain have brought her to.
>
> (IV, vi.)

This daughter is Cordelia—threefold like Lear and Edmund: a person, a principle, and a community.

Before proceding to examine the meaning of Cordelia, however, we must review the ancestry of Edmund to see how *King Lear* completes a process of growth that began with Shakespeare's first ventures on the Elizabethan stage. It will be necessary also to pause over the person of the Fool: a frame of mind apart from Cordelia, in which the dilemma of impossible Hooker and unbearable Hobbes is regarded as insoluble—a nightmare handy-dandy.

PART II

THE PLAY OF 'KING LEAR'
AND SHAKESPEARE'S INNER BIOGRAPHY
UP TO 1606

CHAPTER I

EDMUND'S ANCESTRY

Shakespeare's growing period was a prolonged and exciting one. It began at twenty-five—an age at which in most of our other poets growth has finished—and it continued for another twenty years. Shakespeare's inner biography is a part of Shakespearian studies not yet fully opened out. Findings here must be tentative; the appeal in the last resort is to the reader's intuitions, to his sense of significance and direction in the whole body of Shakespeare's work. Something objective may be established, however, by pursuing in criticism the method so fruitful in archaeology: the placing of related specimens in their series so that the series illuminates and interprets the individual member just as the member adds to and completes the meaning of the series. The history of Edmund in Shakespeare's plays can well form one such instructive series, supplying a fractional insight at least into a part of Shakespeare's mind. It will indicate something of how the new man and the new nature developed.

Edmund's ancestry in the plays runs through Richard III, the Bastard in *King John*, and Falstaff and Hal taken together. The galliards of the comedies are also in the direct line, and Iago as a damaged and degenerate specimen from the tragedies. Edmund, in the view propounded here, is the final statement of the meaning these figures aim at. He is the end-product and they the process. The measure of Shakespeare's inner growth can be gauged when we see in Edmund both Richard III and Henry V epitomized— those opposite poles of the History cycle, which, opposite as they are when considered in the political realm, can both be seen as one when that realm is transcended. In the tragedies this political sphere is transcended. A new dimension is added to it. The Histories are not forgotten, but in the new context that *King Lear* provides they undergo transvaluation.

[a]

RICHARD III

Dr. Tillyard has rightly insisted on the internal unity of Shakespeare's first four histories. They are conceived as a tetralogy. *Richard III* triumphantly concludes Shakespeare's first study in the sixteenth century theory of history, what Dr. Tillyard calls his 'grim and long fidelity to Hall's pattern of cause and effect'.

This pattern might ultimately be based on the biblical text concerning 'the sins of the fathers'. Developed in the late-medieval theme of the falls of princes, it was adjusted by the Tudor historians to a Tudor-propaganda purpose. The intention was to show how the accession of Henry VII restored the health of the commonwealth. The history is official history, and has only to be thus summarily stated to be seen for what it is. Human destiny is confined within a single formula which neither the philosopher nor the plain man would be likely to take at face value. Limited, however, as the scheme is Shakespeare consciously adopted it. With equal deliberacy he schooled himself in devising a Chronicle manner to fit. The idea of Hall provided a strong plot framework—the Divine Comedy of God's revenges. It called out vivid contrasts in mood, fortune, and personality: the internal tensions of people involved in a wave-like rise and fall of fortune, the external tensions of the same people grouping and re-grouping in public conflict on this side and on that as the eddying stream carries them forward from one situation to another. The conception is consciously hieratic in matter and manner. The emotions are vibrant and simple—hate, lust, fear, pity, courage, despair. The verse can attain an almost jet-propelled rigidity and force. The wave-like working of Fortune and Fate in history is introduced into the dramatic form. Shakespeare consciously pursues a principle of emergence. Each play ends with a group destined to grow in importance, to become dominant, and thence decline. The whole movement reaches its climax in *Richard III*. Here the biblical-political theme is fulfilled. Richard is the last, the most formid-able, the wickedest, and the greatest of the unsatisfactory Kings. Around him is arrayed the phalanx of sorrowing queens,—the debris of the preceding plays, kept alive only by the desire to see the completion of God's pattern: His revenge and His justi-fication. The pattern is completed: Richard is vanquished by Henry Richmond, the Henry VII that will be.

Such from one side is the social motivation of the first tetra-logy. There are, of course, other sides. More important than the Tudor propaganda is the other latent content of the cycle. It is by this that the play is knitted into the fabric of Shakespeare's thought and feeling, and thereby made an expression of the thought and feeling of Shakespeare's time. The first tetralogy begins a process which is not completed until *King Lear*, at which point the question of Tudor propaganda is no longer important. Again, it is worth repeating, Shakespeare's charac-ters are not studies in individual psychology only. They are pro-jections of the psychology of Shakespeare's time. Bradley is wrong only in not proceeding to discuss as symbols those characters he sees so intimately as individuals. The rejectors of Bradley are wrong only in pretending that the symbolic content does not also find its most controlled expression in the characters as people.

The axis of the tetralogy is defined by Henry VI on the one hand and Richard III on the other. Henry VI is as nearly blame-less as a king can be. In accordance with sixteenth-century prac-tice he is given a tragic fault (the manner of his marrying the 'she-wolf of France'), but it is merely a token—something as academic as Romeo jilting Rosalind, and as intrinsically meaningless. He behaves throughout the play as the pious, pitiful, Christian-hearted King. Richard is at the opposite extreme. Shakespeare brings the two together in the act which for him would appear to be the most important bit of symbolism in his tragic world—the killing of the King. It is by this act (which he alone of Shakespeare's heroes, before Brutus, is allowed to be guilty of) that Richard crosses a threshold. Such evil, in the history-cycle, is reserved for him alone. By this he severs himself from the group of averagely godless, mediocrely ambitious nobles to which he has hitherto belonged. It is by this that Richard brings to full consciousness what they cannot consciously admit. Richard's isolation might almost be said to be the isolation of one who has become the consciousness of his time. The horror and loathing in which he is held follow as a natural consequence. He reveals to his contemporaries what they really are, what their average social behaviour implies. Paradoxically, Richard exists to tear away the mask his confederate society is wearing. It is only in Richard—the great wearer of masks—that the corruption of his time is made aware of itself. This is the ambiguity of his role: to be the logical outcome of his society, and yet a pariah rejected by that society; a hypocrite, yet more sincere in his self-awareness than those he ruins and deceives; a villain who is also the hero of the chronicle-cycle; a man whose error is to take the average practice of his world, reduce it by analysis to its bare essentials, and erect it, with almost ascetic self-discipline, into a conscious principle of action.

Henry VI is the regulating principle of traditional society. He is mercy, pity, love, human kindness, reinforced by God's ordinating fiat. It is this which Richard kills:

> If any sparke of Life be yet remaining,
> Downe, downe to hell, and say I sent thee thither.
> *Stabs him againe.*
> I that have neyther pitty, love, nor feare,

Indeed 'tis true that Henrie told me of:
For I have often heard my Mother say,
I came into the world with my Legges forward.
Had I not reason (thinke ye) to make hast,
And seeke their Ruine, that usurp'd our Right?
The Midwife wonder'd, and the Women cri'de
O Jesus blesse us, he is borne with teeth,
And so I was, which plainly signified,
That I should snarle, and bite, and play the dogge:
Then since the Heavens have shap'd my Body so,
Let Hell make crook'd my Minde to answer it.
I have no Brother, I am like no Brother:
And this word (Love) which Gray-beards call Divine,
Be resident in men like one another,
And not in me: I am my selfe alone.

(3 *Henry VI*, V, vi.)

Right up to Henry's murder Richard has been a typical member of the Yorkist group. His pre-eminence in fact has been due only to his having the approved qualities of the York family in a larger measure than his brothers. Up to this point, too, the conflict about the throne has been conducted as a dynastic rivalry. There have been rights and wrongs on both sides. No one has made claims as an individual merely. Everything has kept within the limits of the medieval code. The killing of the King marks the transcendence of this code. The dynastic issue is left behind, and it is now a question of Richard's personal ambition. Up to now, from the observer's standpoint, there has been war, bloodshed, treachery, laceration of the body of *Res Publica*: but all as the outcome of debated primogeniture. With Richard the war, bloodshed, treachery and laceration continue: but Richard jettisons the idea that only a discussion of primogeniture is sufficient to justify it. Nothing external is changed or needs to be changed. However, the whole inner meaning of what is happening before our eyes has been transformed completely.

This, I think, is the prime significance Machiavellianism—the mere idea of it—had for the Elizabethans. There is a new sense of the fissuring of man, of a gap between the external and the internal, a possible dichotomy between the social and the spiritual. We can see it even in Hooker's contradiction: man must be thought of as a reasonable creature if we are to justify the unity of law and love, yet for reasons of government it is best to think of him as a law-breaking beast. The new element is not merely the thought of appalling wickedness. It is rather the uneasy feeling that 'wickedness' might be a social advantage. What is morally wrong might be socially expedient, a strong ruler who is bad better than a holy King who is also weak. 'Pity, love and fear' may be governmental handicaps. There is no doubt in the chronicle cycles that Henry VI, by all concerned, is regarded as an irrelevance. Pity, love, and fear are not socially usable as things are. Yet they are the ideal for man, and living together on any other terms than on an assumption of unifying kindness is scarcely reasonable. This honest enigma underlies everything else in the machiavel-figure. It provides the sober basis for what would otherwise be flesh-creeping pantomime. If pity, love, and fear have become socially irrelevant, then are they true, or do greybeards merely say they are divine? If they are not true, then the whole façade of society is a mask. The man conscious of this will be the hypocrite—a man superior in degree of consciousness to his fellows: one able to convince his fellows by his mere existence that they are the mask and he the reality. Behind the mask there is not an angel but a devil—and notwithstanding a more reliable and efficient regulator of *Res Publica*. This man, aware of how things really work, aware of the mockery of moral claims, aware of what men really are motivated by as opposed to what they pretend to themselves, will kill the King.

An indication of the radical nature of this view is the Elizabethan use of the word 'politic', as an adjective to describe the machiavel knave. To any empirical query as to whether machiavellianism works or not, the reply can only be—in politics does anything else work except the 'political'?

The machiavel's is a highly expert social performance. Wearing the social mask he is not detectably different from his neighbour. Being, behind the mask, the deliberate calculator of social means and ends, he is an infallible master of men. Richard has this hypocrisy and psychological insight in a fully-developed form already. As machiavel he analyses the reality behind the pretensions of social man. It is because of the truth of his analysis and the superiority of his insight into the actually operative mechanism of society that he is so successful. The sinister implication of this supreme actor and master psychologist is that he is the reality and his dupes the fiction. He is the fuller consciousness and they the unconscious. Richard is normal in that he comes out from a background of Yorkists whose actions are in all respects like his, and whose standards are the same. Richard is the most typical of the factious lords. Their tacit disregard for the King, their assumption of his irrelevance, is merely the unconscious aspect of what Richard brings to full consciousness when he deliberately kills the King.

Society, then, has actually gone on working with the assumption that 'pity, love, and fear' are irrelevant. The machiavel's advantage is that he is the first to see this, and the first to revise his idea of man so as to become a more efficient social animal. The machiavel knows man better than anyone else. He is abnormal merely in that he does from conscious design what others do from social habit. He is superior in consciousness to his fellows. He is also more successful than they. These three arguments constitute a powerful case. Richard becomes less and less like a creature of melodrama and more and more like a possibility in the actual world.

What is the intrinsically admirable and heroic factor in Richard? It is to be looked for, I think, first in the very superiority of consciousness which makes him more sincerely wicked than the averagely anti-social groups around him; second, in what is an offshoot of this—the fuller exercise of the human prerogative of choice:

Then since the Heavens have shaped my Body so,
Let Hell make crook'd my Minde to answer it.
I have no Brother, I am like no Brother:
And this word (Love) which Gray-beards call Divine,
Be resident in men like one another,
And not in me: I am my selfe alone.

It is this aspect of the machiavel which Shakespeare carries over into the Bastard Falconbridge. The last phrase is almost repeated word for word by him:

And I am I how e'er I was begot.

It is continued obviously in Edmund, too:

I should have been that I am had the maidenliest star in the firmament twinkled on my bastardizing.

And Richard's comparative sincerity in his context is repeated in Edmund's comparative excellence when he is weighed against Gloster's smutty fatuity and doddering superstitiousness.

'I am my selfe alone' would seem to be one of the key-sentiments Shakespeare associates with the type of the New Man. It represents the shift from the absolutes of God and society to the single absolute of the Individual. It is backed, in both Richard's and Edmund's case, by a further bit of motivation which is very important. Richard's wickedness is derived from his malformation at birth (a shape the Heavens are responsible for) and from the ridicule that society bestows on him in consequence. Edmund's bastardy works in the same way as Richard's crookedness. Richard resents both his shape and his position of contemptuous ridicule. He will react therefore against God and man. With both Richard and Edmund we feel that their resentment is understandable. Carried further, we are prepared to feel that their reaction might even be justified. Further still, and we come to the vague notion that Edmund and Richard are somehow *caused*, as they claim to be, by the society they react against. They are both anti-social and an expression of society.

Their corruption is a breaking out of corruption hidden below
the surface, implied in the conduct of the average people around
them, but incapable of being brought to consciousness except
by such experts in self-consciousness as the villains are. The
motivation of the machiavel's wickedness thus reinforces the
impression other aspects of his meaning make—essentially the
impression of the mask and the reality. When the mask falls
away from social man—with his pretensions to pity, love, and
brotherhood, and his actions of unneighbourliness and contempt and hate—it is such a face as Richard's we see, and such a
misshapen form. Richard is society who has slain the hampering
false-consciousness of 'pity, love, and fear'.

The criterion of success which the machiavel adopts is of course
a self-chosen one. It means social success: successful social adapta-
tion. In this field the 'politic' villain is bound to have the advantage. Similarly, in this field, hypocrisy, if it is consummate, is
bound to escape detection. Humanly speaking it is impossible to
differentiate between the truth and the perfect imitation. In his
full maturity, Shakespeare continues to be concerned with this
dilemma. *Othello* translates the political theme of the Chronicles
into an imagery derived from sexual jealousy, but the parable is
the same:

> That one may smile, and smile and be a villain.

And Everyman, 'perplexed in the extreme', will strangle the
Truth adopted by right instinct and natural desire, because
machiavellian consciousness has made it seem only a perfect
imitation.

Othello invokes no dogma whereby we may be assured that
the dilemma is not in fact (as it seems to be) incapable of solution. In the 'Histories', however, Hall's Divine Comedy
guarantees the ultimate frustration of the hypocrite. In the
scheme of God's revenge—a masterly irony—the machiavel
himself is only God's tool. He is a permitted scourge of the
state, but when God's purposes have been served, he must pay

his debts. The theory of history is the same as that we have in the *Mirror*. Shakespeare's Chronicles, too, rely on a divine scale against which to measure the achievements of the machiavel, and thereby reveal the vanity of his pretensions. The criterions assume something more than mere social efficiency.

So in the Chronicle cycle itself the choice Richard heroically makes and maintains is demonstrated to be a wrong choice; it does not pay in the end. Man cannot finally escape his own fullest nature. The false-consciousness of pity and human kindness is a part of that full nature, even if, as things might be, it is socially irrelevant. So we see the answer to the hubristic heroics of Richard's soliloquy on killing the King in Richard's soliloquy when he wakes in a sweat of fright on the eve of the final battle. Richard's conscience has awakened while he has slept.

The full effect of the speech is more than that of a cheap deathbed repentance. It may be a Shakespearian version of Faustus' 'See where Christ's blood streams in the firmament'. But even so it is more than the original and greater—greater through having a central relation to the whole meaning of the cycle, and through giving that meaning a new and exciting turn. Richard has been the man of superior consciousness and has asserted wickedness in this consciousness. He has been the only figure in the cycle capable of full awareness, or of choice. Deplore his choice as we might there is no one his spiritual equal in the four plays. Now the man who is the analyst of the springs of conduct in society, the hypocrite who alone can detect the difference between the mask and the reality, sees in himself a new configuration. He can choose again, in the light of this new awareness, and the amazing thing almost happens: 'Pity, love, and fear' reassert themselves as operative parts of the human unity and Richard is on the brink of readopting them at the higher level of choice—the level of his superior freedom and superior consciousness. It is only because Richard has more often than not been thought of as pantomime villainy and absurd psychology that the importance of this new movement in the machiavel (a

movement Edmund will have, too, 'in spite of his own nature')
has been overlooked:

> Give me another Horse, bind up my Wounds,
> Have mercy Jesu. Soft, I did but dreame,
> O coward Conscience! how dost thou afflict me?
> The lights burne blew. It is not dead midnight.
> Cold fearefull drops stand on my trembling flesh.
> What? do I feare my Selfe? There's none else by.
> *Richard* loves *Richard*, that is, I am I.
> Is there a Murtherer heere? No; yes, I am:
> Then flye; What, from my Selfe? Great reason: why?
> Lest I Revenge. What? my Selfe upon my Selfe?
> Alacke, I love my Selfe. Wherefore? For any good
> That I my Selfe, have done unto my Selfe?
> O no. Alas, I rather hate my Selfe,
> For hatefull Deeds committed by my Selfe.
>
> (*Richard III*, V, iii.)

The two parts of man, social and spiritual, are brought together
again. Both are inside Richard, even if in conflict. They are in no-
one else we see in the Chronicles. It is as if the New Man is in
travail to bring about a new society—better than the old society
with its war and its 'false-consciousness' of the holy King: better
because it will assert a true-consciousness of pity, love, and fear,
and find a social fulfilment for man's instinct towards brotherhood. The miracle, of course, does not happen. Richard becomes
'himself' again: it is the future Henry VII who brings 'order' to
Res Publica.

[b]

KING JOHN

Richard III brings to an end the period of 'grim and long
fidelity' to the theory of history reflected in Hall, the *Mirror*, and
in Tudor propaganda. Immediately, in *King John*, we sense a
swirl of diverse currents uncertain as to the direction in which

they will ultimately set. In verse, characterization, plot, and theme, Shakespeare is reacting against the self-imposed limitations of the early history cycle. One passage will serve to illustrate the dissolving of the old patterns and the suggestion of new. It is the speech of the Bastard Falconbridge when he has discovered the body of Prince Arthur lying dead outside the city walls, and orders Hubert (King John's feudal retainer) to carry it away. Although the Bastard is looking forward down a perspective of future history which will end with the accession of Henry VII, we must remember that Shakespeare has just completed the last chapter in the serial leading up to this event. Shakespeare, so to speak, is looking back over the histories he has just handled:

> Go, beare him in thine armes:
> I am amaz'd me thinkes, and loose my way
> Among the thornes, and dangers of this world.
> How easie dost thou take all *England* up,
> From forth this morcell of dead Royaltie?
> The life, the right, and truthe of all this Realme
> Is fled to heaven: and *England* now is left
> To tug and scamble, and to part by th' teeth
> The un-owed interest of proud-swelling State:
> Now for the bare-pickt bone of Maiesty,
> Doth dogged war bristle his angry crest,
> And snarleth in the gentle eyes of peace:
> Now Powers from home, and discontents at home
> Meet in one line: and vast confusion waites
> As doth a Raven on a sick-falne beast,
> The iminent decay of wrested pompe.
> Now happy he, whose cloake and center can
> Hold out this tempest. Beare away that childe.
>
> (*King John*, IV, iii.)

The pausing and phrasing of the verse is new, and so is the quiet tone of self-communing reflection. It is new, too, in the Histories to come upon a speech which, in its last two lines, can call up so powerfully the overtones of Lear's 'pitiless storm', and, in its first three, challenge the range of Antony's:

Friends, come hither,
I am so lated in the world, that I
Have lost my way for ever.
(*Antony and Cleopatra*, III, ix.)

It is new to find in the Histories the conception of a character suddenly arrested in mid-career, meeting an unexpected and new experience, and undertaking reassessment both of himself and of the world that has so suddenly become unfamiliar. The characters in the early chronicles (Richard's last soliloquy is the only possible exception) never doubt or lose their way. The mental and emotional course they run is as clear as a greyhound track.

The imagery with which Shakespeare handles the central topic is also new: Majesty 'a bare-pickt bone', York and Lancaster destined to indulge in a graceless 'tug and scamble':

Now happy he, whose cloake and center can
Hold out this tempest.

What is especially new is this tacit suggestion of frames of human reference more important than the dynastic scuffle which they enclose, of dignities independent of 'proud-swelling state', of violations greater than 'the decay of wrested pompe'—the suggestion, in other words, of alternative standards of value which will accompany the official version of rights and wrongs and modify its inner emphases. Life, right, and truth are fled to heaven. The free man may be able to wear out the tempest that will surely come, but he will be lucky if he does. 'Heaven' and this 'happy he' seem to stand over in dignity against the momentous 'history' about to be made. It would seem as if Shakespeare, through the Bastard, were looking with a new eye. He sees more, and what he sees is set in a new light.

King John then represents the dissolving of the Chronicle pattern, its break-up and rearrangement. The great change is the acceptance of history as a process not controlled by God, nor subject to the scheme of His revenges. History is no longer divine, and if it continues to be a comedy its humour is sour and grim. The symbolization of this process is apparent in the Bastard's speech over Arthur.

The first tetralogy made Henry VI the soul of society. He represented that essential human kindness which originates society and which society exists to develop. The four plays turn round the question of killing the King, and—in Richard's final soliloquy—we see the King's murderer discovering a Henry VI in his own bosom: it is himself Richard has murdered, and it is this murdered self which will judge and condemn him. Society has tacitly regarded Henry as an irrelevance, and in Richard it has consciously destroyed him. Humanity—in Richard—has chosen to run the state on the assumption of Henry's irrelevance, only to fail: prevented by God, and—claiming the evidence of Richard's soliloquy—by its own nature.

Henry VI portrays the struggle which ends in displacing the holy King. *King John* opens with a usurper already enthroned and foreign powers putting demands before him that he should allow Arthur, the rightful heir, to succeed. Prince Arthur is the same symbol as Henry VI, except that he is a child as well as rightful King. As such he is invested with a double sanctity. The child as the symbol for outraged humanity, ravaged by social strife, haunts Shakespeare's imagination. It reappears in *Macbeth* both as the Bloody Babe and as pity:

> Pitty, like a naked New-borne-Babe,
> Striding the blast, or Heaven's Cherubin hors'd
> Upon the sightlesse Curriors of the Ayre.
>
> (I, vii.)

The faithless dealings of both sides with this regulating principle of civil decency and humanity are fully revealed in the first act. France supports Arthur's right. King John will fight to retain what he possesses. In the bandying of words before resort to arms, John's mother mentions in passing that her son's claim is based on Richard's will. Of course we have just had John's own judgment in a precisely similar contention of primogeniture *versus* father's will. The case of the Bastard and his younger brother made this a central issue. In that instance John decided for primogeniture. Elinor's argument, then, as she knows, is a very feeble one:

> Your strong possession much more than your right.
> Or else it must go wrong with you and me.
>
> *(King John,* I, i.)

The two armies are in front of Angiers, and the townsmen on the wall. Rather surprisingly the high question of principle is referred to the people of the town for decision: whoever they prefer shall be considered rightful ruler. Very cannily, the townsmen prefer not to commit themselves. They will recognize the right of the victor. So the armies engage in battle. Both French and English heralds then appear before the town, each claiming victory. Again the townsmen refrain from rushing in where angels have obviously feared to tread. Their caution is exasperating, and, exasperated, the Bastard hits on a witty plan. He addresses both the Kings:

> Your Royall presences be rul'd by mee,
> Do like the Mutines of Jerusalem,
> Be friends awhile, and both conjoyntly bend
> Your sharpest Deeds of malice on this towne. . . .
>
> *(King John,* II, i.)

Raze the town for its impudence, and then turn to the battle proper once again:

> Then in a moment Fortune shall cull forth
> Out of one side her happy Minion,
> To whom in favour she shall give the day
> And kisse him with a glorious victory:
> How like you this wilde counsell mighty States,
> Smackes it not something of the policie?
>
> *(King John,* II, i.)

The Bastard's policy is liked well, but not however put into execution. It is forestalled by a nicer stroke of policy proposed by

Hubert of Angiers. He suggests that France and England should sink their quarrel, and seal their friendship by marrying England's princess to France's dauphin. The suggestion is adopted immediately. The principle at stake is forgotten. Constance, it is hoped, will be content to have her son made Duke instead of King.

The tone of the act is cynical and casual. Shakespeare is reacting violently against the heavily-charged theological atmosphere of the first tetralogy. The Bastard at the end gives the behaviour of all concerned whatever seriousness it will bear. His comment shows Shakespeare generalizing in a new way and deserves to be quoted in full:

> Mad world, mad kings, mad composition:
> *John* to stop *Arthurs* Title in the whole,
> Hath willingly departed with a part,
> And France, whose armour Conscience buckled on,
> Whom zeale and charitie brought to the field,
> As Gods owne souldier, rounded in the eare,
> With that same purpose-changer, that slye divel,
> That Broker, that still breakes the pate of faith,
> That dayly breake-vow, he that winnes of all,
> Of Kings, of beggers, old men, yong men, maids,
> Who having no externall thing to loose,
> But the word Maid, cheats the poor Maide of that.
> That smooth-fac'd Gentleman, tickling commoditie,
> Commoditie, the byas of the world,
> The world, who of it selfe is peysed well,
> Made to run even, upon even ground;
> Till this advantage, this vile drawing byas,
> This sway of motion, this commoditie,
> Makes it take head from all indifferency,
> From all direction, purpose, course, intent.
> And this same byas, this Commoditie,
> This Bawd, this Broker, this all-changing-word,
> Clap'd on the outward eye of fickle France,
> Hath drawn him from his owne determin'd ayd,
> From a resolv'd and honourable warre,
> To a most base and vile-concluded peace.

And why rayle I on this Commoditie?
But for because he hath not wooed me yet:
Not that I have the power to clutch my hand,
When his faire Angels would salute my palm,
But for my hand, as unattempted yet,
Like a poore begger, raileth on the rich.
Well, whiles I am a begger, I will raile,
And say there is no sin but to be rich:
And being rich, my vertue then shall be,
To say there is no vice but beggerie:
Since Kings breake faith upon commoditie,
Gaine be my Lord, for I will worship thee.

(*King John* II, i.)

The novel thing here is that we can see Shakespeare coming to terms with the machiavel. He is no longer, like Richard, a bogey. He is, on the contrary, engagingly bluff and likeably free from humbug. In the sense that you know and he knows when he is not being strictly honest he might even be considered reliable. The Bastard's speech follows Richard in everything but its tone of carefree 'policie'—the tone handed on to Edmund and inherited by all Shakespeare's machiavels.

First, there is the recognition that the principle symbolized by Henry VI is clearly a false-consciousness. Men's moral pretensions in society are merely pretensions:

And France, whose armour Conscience buckled on,
Whom zeale and charitie brought to the field,
As Gods owne souldier, rounded in the eare,
With that same purpose-changer, that slye divel.

We had to guess at this as an implication in Richard's world. Now it is openly stated. The perception has disengaged itself from the latent content and become only too obvious. Richard took his wickedness to himself, though claiming that society had 'caused' it. The Bastard sees the same wickedness as a clear lesson to be naively drawn from even the most passing acquaintance with the way kings and princes behave. Faithlessness and self-advantage are the social norms, and the country lad who

73

wishes to get on will be well advised to learn the lesson quickly. Men talk about rights and wrongs but act from 'commodity'.

Second, the Bastard is like Richard in being the consciousness of his time. His insight is superior, he is less hampered with self-deceit than his associates—than John, for example, who is not being an ironist when he says:

> Peace be to *France*: if France in peace permit
> Our just and lineall entrance to our owne;
> If not, bleede *France*, and peace ascend to heaven,
> While we Gods wrathful agent doe correct
> Their proud contempt that beats his peace to heaven.
>
> (King John, I, ii.)

Third, like Richard, the Bastard having correctly analysed the practice of society then asserts as a principle what in others is an unreflecting habit:

> Since Kings breake faith upon commoditie,
> Gaine be my lord, for I will worship thee.

Gain here could point us back to Lady Mede of the medieval homily tradition. In the other direction it approximates more closely than anything we have so far encountered to Edmund's 'Thou Nature art my Goddesse'. The difference in the one case is that the Bastard is totally unembarrassed by the homily conscience. In the other case the difference consists in the scope of the election made. Edmund is as unembarrassed as the Bastard. But he is aware that 'Nature' is as far-reaching a choice, and one as fraught with eternal consequences, as Richard's diabolism. 'Nature' is less local than 'Gaine'. Edmund, too, has Richard's sense of an alternative order that he is flouting. The Bastard, as yet, is buoyantly unaware of any higher alternative to the *beau monde* he sees before him. His morality will be that of the emancipated denizen of this sphere. He is too neighbourly to be better, and has no need to be worse, than his neighbour. He might have a proper contempt for his neighbour, but ruefully admits he is much the same sort of man himself.

This suppressed sense of contempt for the society he moves in is a final link with Richard. For even Richard gains sympathy by his Puritan withdrawal from 'the idle pleasures of these days'. This contempt constitutes the machiavel's strongest human appeal. It successfully argues a degree of seriousness and sensitiveness, an intrinsically higher moral potential, than the machiavel's tools possess. This side of Richard is indicated most clearly in his last soliloquy. It comes out, in Falconbridge, in his increased stature after Arthur's death. Shakespeare is enlarging in *King John* on the possibility of redeeming the machiavel: a possibility Richard startles us with in his 'Have mercy, Jesu'.

How this transforming process is conducted in the Bastard we will now examine. It has to do with the link between Falconbridge and Henry V, with that which ties together Henry V and Richard III—hero-villain, and villain-hero.

Broadly speaking, Shakespeare's problem is how to legitimize the illegitimate. Falconbridge is half-way round the circle from Richard. Richard is in one sense socially typical, as the Bastard is. In him the type has no confusedness to mitigate its harmful nature. It is, on the contrary, deliberate and conscious in its operations with the social mechanism. Both the type and the society, however, stand under divine condemnation. Richard is seen in his choice to be of the devil's party.

Falconbridge carries over almost all Richard's sociological symbolism, but Shakespeare does not now put the symbol in a theological frame. So instead of the sombrely diabolical we have a much gayer, more lighthearted figure, a type conceived in terms at first almost purely social. The Bastard arrives at Court from his country-gentleman's home. He brings with him the jaunty mood and brisk manner of the New Man. He is bold, perky, and bouncing. He is rewarded with a knighthood and court favour, the promise of a career open to his talents. At the end of the scene with John and the Queen-Mother we get a vivid sketch of the town-and-courtier type, ending with this comment:

> But this is worshipfull society,
> And fits the mounting-spirit like my selfe;
> For he is but a bastard to the time
> That doth not smoacke of observation,
> And so am I whether I smacke or no:
> And not alone in habit and device,
> Exterior forme, outward accoutrement;
> But from the inward motion to deliver
> Sweet, sweet, sweet poyson for the ages tooth,
> Which though I shall not practice to deceive,
> Yet to avoid deceit I mean to learne;
> For it shall strew the footsteps of my rising.
>
> (*King John*, I, i.)

Falconbridge is determined to be up to date. He flies at convention, at ceremony, pretentiousness, and swagger; the chronicle afflatus of Hubert's verse; the high-flown in the Dauphin's love-making; the pomposity of Austria flaunting in Coeur de Lion's lion-skin. Careless, racy, pert, and outspoken, the Bastard's role in Act I is almost limited to that of *l'enfant terrible*. The impudent mountebank just arriving at Court is barely recognizable in the sober, staunch-hearted hero Falconbridge later becomes.

This is the first step, then, towards legitimizing the illegitimate. The machiavel is made first of all the consciousness of society, given awareness of its 'inward motion'. He is then made into an acceptable and typical social figure, attractive in his 'outward accoutrement'. Instead of a malformed Crookback, we have a handsome young gentleman, as gay as Mercutio, as downright as Berowne, newly arrived from the country, but more than able to hold his own at court: a social type Shakespeare has observed closely. The machiavel is no devil. He belongs instead to the brighter, more desirable circles of London life. His qualities are social assets. Whether they are theological handicaps is not asked.

The second step towards rehabilitation is to give Falconbridge a distinguished and significant parentage. It is no accident that so much is made of his being the natural son to Richard Coeur de Lion. Coeur de Lion is only a name in the play, but at the same time a powerful reminder of the complete king. His reputation dominates the whole of the first act. It accounts for Falconbridge's manliness and his court-favour. It is visibly before us even in France in the lion-skin which Austria wears and which so incenses the Bastard. Coeur de Lion was a legitimate king; he was a strong national champion; he was also a Crusader. He is the only king Shakespeare knows who is completely without flaw. And the Bastard re-incarnates, but in a changed time, the virtues of his father. This new type of hero, both machiavel and man of the world, introduced into the heart of the chronicle matter, is given its greatest sanction by reference to Coeur de Lion, the perfect Englishman.

It might be objected that it is highly fanciful to give Coeur de Lion such importance. Even, however, if we dismiss the fancy, there still remains the substance: the fact that Falconbridge is made into a hero, admitted to be the preliminary sketch for Henry V.

The reconciliation of national villain and national hero in the person of Falconbridge is a main clue to the direction in which Shakespeare is moving. Take away the theological judgment under which Richard stands—assume the social irrelevance of all that Henry VI represents, and immediately it is possible to see the machiavel's qualities in a positive light. They can be necessary to right government: under certain circumstances, even virtues. The changed view will require revision of the view of history taken by Hall and the *Mirror*, and this again Shakespeare proceeds to. A new position is adopted in regard to the central concern of his time—the justness of rebellion.

Falconbridge achieves his fullest stature when he is brought into conjunction with Prince Arthur. The speech over the dead Prince is his noblest insight, and Shakespeare's best poetry in the play. Now that 'the life, the right, and truth of all this realm is fled to heaven' the good man must make the best of what is left. The practical secular virtues—disillusioned, grim, maybe heroic, makeshifts—still remain. They are braced by and centred in a really 'blind' patriotism—a feeling for 'England right or wrong'. The shift of thought involved can be clearly seen in a comparison of the atmosphere of Bosworth Field with that which surrounds the revolt against John. (It is to be remembered that John, like Richard, is a usurper; like Richard, he, too, has killed the King.) The difference is simple—the army marching against Richard is in rightful revolt. The theory justifying it is the classical medieval one that the wicked tyrant may rightly be resisted: the theory of Shakespeare's contemporary catholic world, of those Calvinists who followed John Knox, and of the 1569 rebellion. The theory in *King John* is the theory of the Homilies: nothing justifies rebellion, no wickedness nor wrongfulness in the ruler whatsoever. If the rebellion of Henry Richmond is never brought into relation with the theory of rebellion announced by his granddaughter, it is because Shakespeare's chronicles are Elizabethan content in pre-Elizabethan dress. The upshot of this new turn of thought is to make those who are outraged at the killing of Arthur rebels: and as such they cannot be justified. The Bastard is, however, on John's side, and England's. He will oppose the rebels and the French who are supporting them. There is nothing admirable left in John. He is a sick man and a craven. The safety of England depends on Falconbridge. Falconbridge's new ethic, now that Arthur is dead, strikes a note that persists, with differences, in *Macbeth* and *Lear*:

> Be stirring as the time, be fire with fire,
> Threaten the threatner, and out-face the brow
> Of bragging horror.
>
> (*King John*, V, i.)

Fortitude, awareness of what 'the times' require, and patriotism —these are the cardinal virtues of the new hero. And there is no sanctity left in Kingship. Kings will have to prove themselves men as good as the Bastard.

We might briefly follow the course of Shakespeare's thought

on rebellion in *Henry IV* and *King Lear*. It indicates as well as anything else the spiral of his inner biography.

The new thought in *King John*—that the unity and integrity of England is the overriding moral claim—continues in the tetralogy that follows. The key-occasion when this theory is tested is, of course, the rebellion in *Henry IV, Part 2*, and how it is handled by Prince John of Lancaster. The general situation is a replica of that in *King John*. In point of right, Henry IV's claim to the throne is disputable. The rebels have mixed motives, but in addition to the injustices they themselves have suffered, they claim also to be rebelling on principle: Mortimer's line is the rightful line, not Henry's. In the person of the Archbishop of York the Church supports the rebellion. In the parley he holds with the rebels Prince John admits the justice of their demands. He even promises full redress of their grievances. On this under-standing the rebels disperse their forces. Immediately Prince John orders the seizure of the leaders and the pursuit and slaughter of their followers. The treachery is obvious, and neither Shakespeare nor any reasonable man—however often he had heard Elizabeth's homilies—could approve it. Prince John is a dutiful agent of the state but also a scoundrel. Morality however is irrelevant when the peace of *Res Publica* is threatened;

God and not we hath safely fought to-day,

Prince John piously comments, and it is the theology of the Elizabethan settlement. In putting it on record Shakespeare behaves without malice or irony. But for Shakespeare, as for any-one else, it cannot represent a final view. It is an official morality which Shakespeare is soon to discard.

In discarding it Shakespeare returns to what might appear to be the *Richard III* position all over again. In form, it is the same. Shakespeare returns to the theology which can find a means to put complete societies under judgment. The content of the theology, however, has undergone development.

King Lear provides the second replica. The legitimate English rulers are wicked and are being assailed. The case is put in its extreme form: the assailants are being helped by a foreign army. Albany who knows the rulers to be wicked and the regime to be unjust has to choose between joining the rebels or fighting on behalf of Goneril and Regan. His final decision—after grave doubts—is to oppose Cordelia:

ALBANY: Our very loving sister, well be-met:
          Sir, this I heard, the King is come to his daughter
          With others, whom the rigour of our state
          Forc'd to cry out: where I could not be honest
          I never yet was valiant, for this business
          It touches us, as France invades our land,
          Not bolds the King, with others whom I fear,
          Most just and heavy causes make oppose.
BASTARD: Sir, you speak nobly.
REGAN: Why is this reason'd?
GONERIL: Combine together 'gainst the enemy:
          For these domestic and particular broils,
          Are not the question here.
ALBANY: Let's then determine
          With th' ancient of war on our proceeding.

                                     (V, i.)

Albany joining Goneril and Regan is the Bastard siding with John rather than keeping faith with dead Arthur; or he is Prince John (and Hal) doing the work of *Res Publica* in the confidence that only her security is right: Albany, of course, has the moral advantage of Prince John in that he does intend a full pardon to Lear and Cordelia once he has scattered their army.

Albany, however, is only a detail in the general pattern of *King Lear*. In terms of that pattern there can be no doubt that his decision is wrong. Cordelia's cause is just, the invading army a righteous one, rebellion necessary. In *King Lear*, as in the earliest Chronicles, God is again working in history, though in a different way. The machiavel is no longer the highest consciousness of his time. Edmund in this respect has to give way to Edgar and Cordelia.

[c]

HENRY IV, PARTS I AND 2

The Henry IV plays were written before the Essex rebellion. They are not, therefore, the creations of a particular crisis. They reflect none of the turmoil which that rupture of the uneasy Elizabethan compromise may be assumed to have precipitated. In view of the textual history of the plays, this is an ironical fact. Shakespeare was never further from questioning the Elizabethan establishment than in part of the Lancastrian cycle, and yet it was part of the Lancastrian cycle that panicking officials censored on account of its chance connection with incendiary literature made use of by the Essex faction. *Henry IV, Parts 1 and 2* is neither so serious-minded as the first tetralogy, nor so profound as the tragedies. This is not to say that the second tetralogy marks a falling off in dramatic power when compared with the first: quite the contrary is the case. The distinction might best be made in this way. In the first tetralogy Shakespeare is consciously concerned with an intellectual thesis that actively controls his material. In the second tetralogy he has lost interest in this thesis, and at the same time no scheme of comparable relevance or individual concern has presented itself. The Prince Henry plays are a true growing period, but intellectualism in historical presentation does not in them play so active a part. The energy devoted to maintaining a thesis flows therefore into other channels. It is made available to support an even greater proliferation of fully realized individuals; and, it is used to fill in a broader and differently conceived 'England'. The Prince Henry plays show Shakespeare's powers as a playwright more fully developed than ever before. They may be, as plays, better than either *Richard III* or *King Lear* (they are certainly better than *King John*). Spirits, however, are not finely touched but to fine issues. The present contention is merely that

Shakespeare's spirit in *Henry IV* is not finely touched because the issues in the play are not such as call to him profoundly. In what follows, therefore, there is no intention of doing full justice to the plays as a whole. Only the 'issues' in the plays will be isolated, and these only as they are recognizable links in the series stretching from Richard Crookback to Edmund.

Discussion of the plays turns round the relations of Falstaff and Hal. As a further preliminary we might be allowed to describe at the outset the assumptions which govern the discussion following. It is admitted, with audiences from Shakespeare's day to ours and with critics from Hazlitt to Bradley, that Falstaff walks off with both parts of *Henry IV*. It is admitted, too, with critics up to and including Coleridge, and with Dr. Tillyard and Prof. Dover Wilson of recent commentators, that Shakespeare's intention was to make Hal the real hero of both parts, and Falstaff the deservedly rejected, utterly discredited, villain. It is suggested that both admissions are compatible: Hal is the end of the old period in Shakespeare's development, Falstaff the portent of a new; Hal is Shakespeare's tired consciousness, Falstaff the sign of meanings growing unconsciously; Hal is part of a dying Shakespeare, Falstaff the promise of rebirth.

Henry IV, Parts 1 *and* 2 takes over the assumptions that are left in *King John* once Prince Arthur is dead. Shakespeare resigns himself to the situation in which:

> The life, the right, and truthe of all this Realm
> Is fled to Heaven; and England now is left
> To tug and scamble. . . .

Prince Arthur is, I think, a private symbol for Shakespeare as well as an objective figure in history. In relation to Shakespeare's inner biography he stands for the tap-root to a certain moral ideal of human nature and society which was necessary to provide Shakespeare's imagination with its richest food. The death of Arthur cuts that tap-root. It indicates an effort on Shakespeare's part to dissociate himself from the ideal, and find accommodation in a world where the human decencies have no functional relevance.

In this connection we might refer to the general impression made by the Prince Henry plays—the impression of a comparative lack of depth and lack of vision. The conception of the character of Prince Henry himself is often made responsible for this impression. More properly, however, the source should be looked for in something pervasive of the plays as a whole.

In *Richard III* and *King John* Shakespeare has educated us to look for two main things in his work. The first is a frame of absolute moral values that embraces both the individual and society and yet transcends them; something that provides a basis for private goodness, that implies a norm for the public institutions of the State, that is ultimately vested however in God as a simple categorical obligation. Shakespeare (like Solovyov) apprehends this inclusive good as a threefold thing: pity, which determines one's right relation to one's neighbour; love, which can be a private victory over 'shame' in the individual's life; fear, which is a regulating sense of awe in all our dealings with the values. The second touchstone we have been taught to expect follows logically from the first. It consists in a single dominating figure who is aware on the one hand of the ideal demands and, on the other, of the unideal actualities of society. This central figure, in view of his superior consciousness, is the hero of the play. He is forced to choose between alternatives. He may choose one way or the other, and, in virtue of the choice be a Richard or a Falconbridge.

In *Henry IV* the frame of 'pity, love, and fear' has completely vanished. The world we see is one that has disintegrated into mutually exclusive spheres—the worlds of the Court (Prince John of Lancaster), of the tavern, of Shallow's Gloucestershire, of the rebellious lords: frigid opportunism, riotous irresponsibility, fatuous inconsequence, quarrelsome 'honour'—with no common term except the disease of each. 'England' is sometimes said to be the heroic composite thing that is portrayed. If this is so, it is an England seen in her most unflattering aspects—an England pervaded throughout court, tavern, and country retreat by pitiless fraud. Pity is the reconciling sweetness that the world of the plays most lacks. It is the absence of pity in Hal's dealings with Falstaff that explains the 'romantic' recoil from the Prince. (The age of the romantics rediscovered pity.) We can readily admit that the newly-crowned King must stop being the old prince; but only sophistry could see proper 'kindliness' in the manner of his dealings with Falstaff at the end of *Henry IV*, *Part 2*. We might admit, with Dr. Tillyard, that the Prince is Shakespeare's attempt to construct a good man on Aristotelian norms; but we should still insist that such a conception, with its absence of pity, represents a real loss in comparison with the unconscious Christian norms of Richard and Falconbridge. It is Falstaff, of course, who makes the great appeal to the spectator's sense of pity. But Falstaff himself is the most pitiless creature in the play—Falstaff deceiving Shallow, recruiting his Gloucestershire yokels, ruining Mistress Quickly, despising Hal; predatory Falstaff about to swoop on the body politic and make it his new prey. The absence of pity makes for spiritual incoherence in the world of the play as a whole, and for lack of moral integrity in the individuals that compose it. Even inside the separate spheres there is no cohesion. Hotspur quarrels with Glendower, Northumberland's sickness leads to his son's defeat, Poins and the Prince have purposes between them at odds with those of their fellows, the devotion of Mistress Quickly and Bardolph to Falstaff gains them no equivalent return from him, Hal and his father are estranged, John of Lancaster is distinct from both even after the family reconciliation. No character in the plays provides a satisfying point of rest—unless for rest we turn from the smaller confusions of Northumberland, Hotspur, Bolingbroke, Prince John, Mistress Quickly, Shallow, Doll Tearsheet, Poins and Hal, to lose ourselves in perplexity among the roomier contradictions of Falstaff. If anything unifies this congeries of unharmonized monads it is 'Commodity'—commodity unavowed by any, but duly observed by all, commodity acted upon unconsciously, the condition that ensures its greatest efficiency as a motive for conduct.

Richard III and *King John* both revolve round a dominant figure who in his own consciousness experiences the polarity of 'commodity' and 'pity'. It goes without saying that the Prince Henry plays cannot include such a consciousness. Prince Arthur is dead, and Shakespeare knows it. No one in *Henry IV*, however, can be permitted the same awareness. The world must now go on as if he had never existed. The problem is to find a makeshift ideal which can stand in the 'tempest' of 'the times' now that 'the life, the right, and truth' are departed. Such a makeshift Shakespeare invents in Prince Hal.

It is a critical commonplace that Hal is Shakespeare's ideal king in the Chronicle plays. He is not, however, ideal absolutely. He is the best possible within the limits perceived by Falconbridge as conditioning all future affairs of England. He is not absolutely ideal in one sense for the simple reason that his legitimacy is debatable—and the debate comes to a head in the reign of his son. He is not ideal in another sense, because he is conceived on lines less absolutely heroic, less in spiritual scope, than either Richard or the Bastard. Hal has not their profound consciousness, their social and moral insight, nor does *Henry IV* in Shakespeare's biography represent the period of his deepest social and moral concern. Falconbridge sees 'Commodity' at work in society, and determines to arrange his conduct accordingly; he experiences also the spiritual tremor of the final departure of pity. Hal is incapable of either. Both the 'Commodity' speech, and the speech over dead Arthur are great poetry. *Henry IV* has nothing that could be put beside them.

Hal's most serious moment is the scene in which he is at the bedside of the dying Bolingbroke. What is most striking in this scene is the chronicle-familiarity of the issues raised, and the absence of imaginative reverberation:

> Why doth the Crowne lye there, upon his Pillow,
> Being so troublesome a Bed-fellow?
> O pollish'd Perturbation! Golden Care!
> That keep'st the ports of Slumber open wide
> To many a watchful Night: sleepe with it now,
> Yet not so sound, and halfe so deepely sweete
> As hee whose Brow (with homely Biggen bound)
> Snores out the Watch of Night.
>
> (2 *Henry IV*, IV, v.)

Every good in *Henry IV* is a damaged good. Hal's moralizing seems to reflect the traditional medieval doctrine of kingly responsibility, and consequent 'care'. It might recall Henry VI's soliloquy:

> Gives not the Hawthorne bush a sweeter shade
> To Shepheards, looking on their silly Sheepe,
> Then doth a rich Imbroider'd Canopie
> To Kings, that feare their Subjects treacherie?
> O yes, it doth; a thousand fold it doth.
> And to conclude, the Shepherds homely Curds,
> His cold thinne drinke out of his Leather Bottle,
> His wonted sleepe, under a fresh trees shade,
> All which secure, and sweetly he enjoyes,
> Is farre beyond a Princes Delicates:
> His Viands sparkling in a Golden Cup,
> His bodie couched in a curious bed,
> When Care, Mistrust, and Treason waits on him.
>
> (3 *Henry VI*, II, v.)

The uneasiness of the crowned head, however, in Hal's speech is due to the guilt attaching to the method whereby the crown was come by. Hal's father takes up the tale in the same scene:

> Heaven knowes, my Sonne,
> By what by-pathes, and indirect crook'd-wayes
> I met this Crown: and I my selfe know well
> How troublesome it sate upon my head.
>
> (2 *Henry IV*, IV, v.)

For Henry Bolingbroke the crown had been 'an honour snatched with boistrous hand'. Both the crown and its legacy of trouble are to be handed on to Hal: and Hal cannot expect an easy time:

> Thou art not firme enough, since greefes are greene:
> And all thy Friends, which thou must make thy Friends,
> Have but their stings, and teeth, newly tak'n out.
>
> (2 *Henry IV*, IV, v.)

Even Henry's holy crusade was a mere strategy by foreign adventures to avoid or quieten domestic dissatisfactions. His last advice to his son is to pursue a similar policy:

> Therefore (my *Harry*)
> Be it thy course to busie giddy Mindes
> With Forraigne Quarrels: that Action hence borne out,
> May waste the memory of the former days.
>
> (2 *Henry IV*, IV, v.)

This, presumably, is the reality behind the glory of *Henry V*. We are back, in this interview between father and son, at the level of King John and the Queen-mother:

KING JOHN: Our strong possession, and our right for us.
ELINOR: Your strong possession much more than your right,
          Or else it must go wrong with you and me,
          So much my conscience whispers in your ear,
          Which none but heaven, and you, and I, shall heare.

> (*King John*, I, i.)

Hal's last words to his father concern 'strong possession'; neither Heaven, nor conscience are mentioned; and right is equated to possession:

> My gracious Liege:
> You wonne it, wore it: kept it, gave it me,
> Then plaine and right must my possession be;
> Which I, with more then with a Common paine,
> 'Gainst all the World will rightfully maintaine.
>
> (2 *Henry IV*, IV, v.)

The world of the early chronicles was capable of reference to wider issues than the frame of state-expediency can include. The scene between Hal and his father, taken together with John of

Lancaster's handling of the rebels, points to the complete banishment of the values that gave the earlier world its depth and breadth. Now that the internal order of 'pity, love, and fear' is gone, there is only the external order to fall back on, the officialese of Elizabeth's Homilies to be repeated, with their non-theology that maintains Tudor possession at all costs, their no-morality that claims rebellion is always wicked. It was idle of the Elizabethan censor to be afraid of the implications of *Henry IV*. It represents a view of history which makes sedition impossible. Whatever is, is right, provided it is strong: right in a makeshift way, to be tested by the secular standard of success, justified by its ability to hold what it has: the right, the life, the truth of all this realm is fled to heaven.

These then are the limits to the ideal. But within these limits Hal is still Shakespeare's hero. He carried on Shakespeare's conscious intent to come to terms with contemporary social reality. After *King John*, we said, Kings would have to prove themselves men as good as the Bastard. Hal is meant to be such a man and such a King. In his person (Bolingbroke suspected Hal of being a changeling) the Bastard ascends the legitimate throne.

Part of the Bastard's qualities are inherited by Hotspur. (In Commodity's world everyone is pretty much the same in private, however they may take opposite sides in public.) Hotspur has the rude boisterousness of Falconbridge; his impatience with humbug, high-falutin verse, and romantic love-making; his bluntness, impudence, and vigour. Hotspur has also Falconbridge's gift for the satirical mimicking of effete social types. Hotspur, too, is a New Man. His cult of 'honour' cannot be mistaken for a knightly ideal of 'maydenhead'. For Hotspur war is a game really played for the sidestakes of 'reputation'.

The similarity of Hotspur and Hal is derivable from their common source in Falconbridge. Hotspur is also, however, a foil for Hal. The contrast between them is in a sense the contrast between Falconbridge in the first act of *King John*, and

Falconbridge in the rest of the play: with the omissions, in each case, that have been already noted. Hotspur has no insight into 'Commodity', Hal no moral realization of pity, love, and fear' departing from the sphere of history. The sharing of Falconbridge between Hotspur and Hal is not, however, a final scission:

> Percy is but my Factor, good my Lord,
> To engrosse up glorious Deedes on my behalfe.
> (1 *Henry IV*, III, ii.)

Hotspur is Hal's proxy on the field of chivalry as Falstaff is on Gadshill. As befits a prince, Hal does none of the labouring in either case. He appears at the right time to rob both champions of their spoil. Hal is never involved directly either in the 'tug and scamble', the shady work of Eastcheap, or in the pot-hunting for 'honour'. These are implications—the indignities in which his dignity is rooted. Hal's inclusiveness as the perfect all-rounder must be asserted, but his princeliness must also be maintained. He is the distilled essence of the new humanity, not its crude original forms. Vernon paints his finest portrait:

> I saw young *Harry* with his Bever on,
> His Cushes on his thighes, gallantly arm'd,
> Rise from the ground like feathered *Mercury*.
> (1 *Henry IV*, IV, i.)

Mercury is a god, and mercury is quicksilver. Just as the lack of coherence in the world of the play as a whole is compensated for by an amazing vividness and surface life in the individual components, Hal's lack of inner depth is balanced by a brilliant range and facility of gesture. But not even Shakespeare's virtuosity can dispel the impression of hollowness in the end. Hal remains a façade.

In Hal the figure of the machiavel undergoes a further and most surprising development. The full machiavel strategy is retained, but it is machiavellism turned inside out. Hal is the sheep in wolf's clothing, a machiavel of goodness:

I know you all, and will a while uphold
The unyoak'd humor of your idlenesse . . .
So when this loose behaviour I throw off,
And pay the debt I never promised;
By how much better then my word I am,
By so much shall I falsifie mens hopes,
And like bright Mettall on a sullen ground,
My reformation glittering o're my fault,
Shall shew more goodly, and attract more eyes,
Then that which hath no foyle to set it off.
Ile so offend, to make offence a skill,
Redeeming time, when men thinke least I will.

(1 *Henry IV*, I, ii.)

This is a bold attempt to enlist the machiavel in the ranks of virtue. But virtue itself wilts when it is made the object of a machiavellian strategy. It sinks to reputation, and that to the acclamation of one's dupes. The externals have again replaced the internals. To pseudo-goodfellowship in Hal must be added pseudo-morality.

Hal's soliloquy brings us, of course, to the question of his relation to Falstaff. Prof. Dover Wilson is right at least in insisting on the connection between Hal in this speech and Hal at the end of *Henry IV, Part* 2, rejecting his one-time companion.

Hal, we have said, is Shakespeare's tired consciousness, Falstaff Shakespeare's unconscious. Hal is a polished Falconbridge: gay, courageous, patriotic, acquainted with every sort of man, the winner—in open competition—of all the social prizes; excellent in the tap-room, on the battlefield, in the councils of state. There can be no doubt that he is intended for a new model King, a sixteenth-century paragon. The model itself, however, we have suggested, falls short of the absolute ideal Shakespeare has educated us already to expect. In the preceding chronicle plays the issues raised had been wider: Is the King right or wrong? Is the state just or unjust?—Even in the person of Jack Cade these questions are posed. In *Henry IV, Parts* 1 *and* 2 the questions are reduced and vulgarized: Is the King strong or

weak? Is the state secure or insecure? Shakespeare's first machiavel descried the actual mechanics of human motive in society.
Richard appreciated the importance of self-interest, approved
it, and decided on a ruthless employment of his intelligence to
encompass the ends proposed by appetite. 'Pity, love, and fear'
he dismissed as irrelevancies. But Richard was wicked. Shakespeare insists that his choice was wrongful. Then the machiavel,
and the society he interprets, is submitted to a process of whitewashing. This process ends in the machiavel of goodness, Prince
Hal. Hal is no longer aware that society might be wicked. He
espouses the aims and the means of the society to hand, he
equips himself to be good in accordance with the terms of the
State he will ultimately govern:

> Ile so offend, to make offence a skill.

This line gives the masterly essence of the new morality. Crude
machiavellism says that the end justifies the means. Refined
machiavellism merely says: Let what you can do indicate what
you can do better: technique is the thing, let the ends look after
themselves. It is the attitude underlying sixteenth-century capitalist development (in war, mining, and trade) and the attitude
implied in the scientific programmes which grew out of that
development.

This twofold attitude to Hal involves a twofold attitude to
Falstaff. In so far as we see Hal as the model chronicle-hero, in
accordance with Shakespeare's intention, Falstaff will then be
the decided villain of the plays. If we tend to criticize Shakespeare's model as an inadequate ideal, compared with his early
chronicle plays and with his later tragedies, then Falstaff will
tend to acquire merit (deserved or undeserved) from his rejection. Critics have followed both paths. There has been a 'Hal
party' and a 'Falstaff party'. The point missed in the debate has
been, I think, the most important one: that Falstaff and Hal
belong together, that they can be accepted together or rejected
together. Shakespeare in *Henry IV* is a Shakespeare in transition.

It is impossible to deny that he has already moved on in the Hal plays themselves. And he is still moving. As Hal turns away from Falstaff Shakespeare himself turns away from Hal.

In what sense can we say Falstaff is a villain? Coleridge was in no doubt and gives an almost convincing answer. Coleridge groups Falstaff with Richard III and Iago:

> The characters of Richard III, Iago, and Falstaff, were the characters of men who reverse the order of things, who place intellect at the head whereas it ought to follow like geometry, to prove and confirm. . . . Falstaff not a degraded man of genius, like Burns, but a man of degraded genius, with the same sense of superiority to his companions, fastened himself on a young Prince, to prove how much his influence on an heir apparent could exceed that of statesmen. With this view he hesitated not to practise the most contemptuous of all characters: an open and professed liar: even his sensuality was subservient to his intellect, for he appeared to drink sack in order to have occasion to show his wit. One thing, however, worthy of observation was . . . the final contempt such a character deserved, and received from the young King.

It is not the popular view of Falstaff, though a similar view has been recently revived by Dr. Tillyard and Prof. Dover Wilson. It answers to something really sinister, however, in Falstaff's make-up, something not allowed to reveal itself as menacing until the old King is dead:

> Boote, boote, Master *Shallow*, I know the young King is sick for mee. Let us take any mans Horsses: the Lawes of England are at my command'ment. Happie are they which have been my Friendes: and woe unto my Lord Chiefe Justice.
>
> (2 *Henry IV*, V, iii.)

This is an unusual piece of self-revelation. Malice, vindictiveness, and overweening arrogance have not hitherto displayed themselves so openly in Falstaff. Nor, up to now, has he shown any sign of the fatal defect now apparent—the taking of himself seriously. This breach in his cynicism we are not prepared for, and not quite able to stomach. Falstaff sees the throne vacated for himself to occupy—a prospect not likely to lead to any more

fun. Coleridge and Dr. Tillyard are right to take Falstaff
seriously.

Shakespeare does not let us see Hal putting Falstaff aside until
he has first shown us Falstaff contemptuously rejecting the
Prince. Falstaff's *hubris* consists in assuming he will be as free
in the court as he is with the household of Master Shallow:

> It is a wonderfull thing to see the semblable Coherence of his mens
> spirits, and his: They, by observing of him, do beare themselves like
> foolish Justices: Hee, by conversing with them, is turn'd into a Justice-
> like Servingman. Their spirits are so married in Conjunction, with the
> participation of Society, that they flocke together in consent, like so
> many Wilde-Geese. If I had a suit to Mayster *Shallow*, I would humour
> his .nen, with the imputation of beeing neare their Mayster. If to his
> Men, I would curry with Maister *Shallow*, that no man could better
> command his Servants. It is certaine, that either wise bearing, or
> ignorant Carriage is caught, as men take diseases, one of another:
> therefore, let men take heed of their Companie. I will devise matter
> enough out of this *Shallow*, to keep Prince *Harry* in continuall Laugh-
> ter, the wearing out of sixe Fashions (which is foure Tearmes) or two
> Actions, and he shall laugh with *Intervallums*. O it is such that a Lye
> (with a slight Oath) and a jest (with a sadde brow) will doe, with a
> Fellow, that never had the Ache in his shoulders. O you shall see him
> laugh, till his Face be like a wet Cloake, ill laid up.
>
> (2 *Henry IV*, V, i.)

It is quite clear that we need not give Falstaff more quarter than
he gives Shallow, or would give Hal. Where Commodity is
King it is each for himself.

The speech shows Falstaff too as a machiavel (Coleridge's
grouping of Falstaff with Richard and Iago points in the same
direction). The spread of machiavellism in the play, like the
partition of Falconbridge into Hotspur and Hal, is not to be
wondered at. 'Commodity' involves the essential alikeness of
the various competitors in its world. Hal and Falstaff are allo-
tropic forms of 'Commodity'. Where there is no organic unity
in society, differences of status and function are absolute differences. A change of status necessitates a change of dress. Falstaff,
then, must be discarded like a worn-out suit. Hal is right, of

course. He cannot share his throne, and remain a renaissance Prince. Much less can he admit Riot, in the person of Falstaff, to usurp his place: Henry Bolingbroke's vision in that event would come true with a vengeance:

> Downe Royall State: All you sage Counsailors, hence:
> And to the English Court, assemble now
> From ev'ry Region, Apes of Idlenesse.
> Now, neighbor-Confines, purge you of your Scum:
> Have you a Ruffian that will sweare? drinke? dance?
> Revell the night? Rob? Murder? and commit
> The oldest sinnes, the newest kinde of wayes?
> Be happy, he will trouble you no more:
> England shall double gild his treble guilt.
> England shall give him Office, Honor, Might:
> For the Fift *Harry*, from curb'd Licence pluckes
> The muzzle of Restraint; and the wilde Dogge
> Shall flesh his tooth in every Innocent.
>
> (2 *Henry IV*, IV, ii.)

Falstaff would be that 'wild dog', there is no doubt. Falstaff can be no more tolerated in court than Lear's rioting can be borne in the 'graced palace' of Goneril and Regan. From the point of view of responsible governors both old men are equally disgraceful ruffians: and both deserve banishment.

The parallel between the rejection of Falstaff and the banishment of Lear by his daughters is a fair one. If it is nonsense to plead that Lear's rejection was justified that is because of a development in Shakespeare's world-view beyond the impasse of *Henry IV*. *King Lear* provides a synthesis which resolves the unresolved oppositions of the Hal tetralogy. It gives the ground for a true solution of the false alternatives of Hal or Falstaff. We shall return to this solution. Meantime it is important to understand what moral and intellectual situation confronts us in the last scene of *Henry IV*, *Part 2*. It is equally important to see the real reference *Henry IV*, *Parts 1 and 2* makes to Shakespeare's contemporary world.

The rejection of Falstaff by Hal is an allegory. Behind that allegory is the concrete world of Elizabeth and her England. The twin forces in the sixteenth century state—each one needing the other, both in an uneasy state of counterpoise, capable of clashing as well as collaborating—were Appetite and Authority. In the rejection scene Hal and my Lord Chief Justice stand for Authority; Falstaff is Appetite, wonderfully enlarged, marvellously self-confident, a 'bolting hutch of beastliness', naïve and unashamed. Authority in Elizabeth's world lived and was sustained by Appetite. It could not have lasted in the world of Appetite, however, if it had not been strong. Authority therefore was, in the end, Power. Power was needed in the Tudor world (as in Henry V's) to centralize, organize, canalize, concentrate, and sometimes curb Appetite; to check it and give it more adequate goals—Spanish treasure fleets instead of merchant men on Gadshill, the Grand Lease of the Prince Bishop's coal mines instead of Mistress Quickly's bed linen. Falstaff's world is a symbol of the unofficial side of Elizabeth's reign. There was always also the official sphere of order and ceremony and decorum the buccaneer and entrepreneur readily fell in with. But the real work of the realm was done on the high seas by the buccaneers, in the coal mines and salt-beds and glass and brass manufactories by the entrepreneur: an unofficial realm Elizabeth could only recognize in private, when the attention of the rest of Europe was distracted elsewhere.

The high life of Elizabeth's monopolist-courtiers we see in *Henry IV*, *Part* I, when Hotspur and Glendower are quarrelling over the carving-up of the Kingdom. The unvarnished version is Falstaff and his retainers at their shady business. Appetite monstrous and unabashed, as plausible as it is unlimited, strides through London and the English countryside in Falstaff's person. The protective camouflage of the official world he does not need. His cynicism, as Bradley points out, pierces to the bottom of truth, honour, law, patriotism, duty, courage, war, religion. And everything at bottom, he sees—as the machiavel does—is self-preservation: 'What, ye rogues, young men must live.' His is the vitality and consciencelessness of Hawkins on the high seas. Hal, as Authority, is Elizabeth. Elizabeth had her unruly brigandage which nourished, supported, and sometimes clumsily clashed with her 'Order'—Drakes who flouted her with her silent permission, Essexes who presumed too far on the strength of the Queen's favour and met with sudden rebuff. Hal throws off Falstaff in order to be a more effective King: Elizabeth put away the flesh to be all the more effectively the Virgin Queen. Elizabeth's asceticism, of course, had its limits. Love of pomp, display, flattery, and money she indulged to the full. Hal's moral stance also has its limits, the limits of the necessity to be strong in possession of his throne, and the original limits of his entire manoeuvre to make reformation a means rather than an end:

> My reformation, glitt'ring o're my fault,
> Shall show more goodly, and attract more eyes,
> Than that which hath no foyle to set it off.
> Ile so offend, to make offence a skill,
> Redeeming time when men thinke least I will.

What we have called Authority (or Power) and Appetite Dr. Tillyard calls Order and Disorder (or Riot) and accounts for *Henry IV, Parts 1 and 2* in these terms. Dr. Tillyard makes an absolute distinction between the two. Order is a real absolute value, Riot a real immorality. Hal turns his back irrevocably on Riot and is converted to the party of My Lord Chief Justice—*Justitia*. The view proposed here as an alternative to Dr. Tillyard's makes no such absolute difference between Hal and Falstaff. The opposition into which they are thrown is an appearance rather than a reality. When Hal moves from Eastcheap to the Court, from Falstaff to My Lord Chief Justice, he is merely leaving the unofficial sphere of Elizabethan life for the official sphere. The two are different, and require different habits. But the difference is not essentially a moral difference. It is a difference of social function. On the view proposed here Authority (or Power) and Appetite occupy the same plane. Both are essential to the running of the Elizabethan state. Equally immoral, both collaborate to maintain an iniquitous world. The Elizabethan state was such a world, a corrupt society. The view taken here is the same, I think, as Gerard Winstanley's, and the same that Shakespeare comes to in *King Lear*. By the 'flesh' Winstanley meant (a) the unruly, pitiless, selfish passions, and (b) the official arm of the State—its laws, penalties, rules, and regulatory manipulations of Appetite. Winstanley, that is, could see both Authority and Appetite as aspects of the same thing, and condemn both. Winstanley, I think, was right, and Shakespeare, I think, makes a similar judgment in *King Lear*. There Appetite and Authority coalesce in the persons of Goneril and Regan, the twin queens of England.

Hal and Falstaff, then, go together. They are to be accepted together, or rejected together. Certainly Hal's rejection of Falstaff must not be regarded as more significant than his long association with the rogue. It need not even be regarded as a final rejection. Prof. Dover Wilson has laboured successfully to show that Hal in the rejection scene is not being so hard on the old man as less percipient critics have led us to believe. There is also Falstaff's last word on the business (which Prof. Dover Wilson does not take so seriously as other parts of the text):

> Master Shallow, do not you grieve at this: I shall be sent for in private to him: Looke you, he must seeme thus to the world: fear not your advancement: I will be the man yet, that shall make you great. . . . This that you heard, was but a colour.
>
> (2 *Henry IV*, V, v.)

Such a 'colour' would be very credible to 'an Elizabethan audience'. It was Elizabeth's own way of dealing with her brigandage.

Analysis leaves us, then, with symbols of Power and Appetite as the keys to the play's meaning: Power and Appetite, the two sides of Commodity. The world is disunited and corrupt at heart. Corruption and disunity spread, too, through the whole body politic. The England depicted in *Henry IV*, *Part* 1 *and* 2 is neither ideally ordered nor happy. It is an England, on the one side, of bawdy-house and thieves'-kitchen, of waylaid merchants, badgered and bewildered Justices, and a peasantry wretched, betrayed, and recruited for the wars; an England, on the other side, of the chivalrous wolf-pack of Hotspur and Douglas, and of state-sponsored treachery in the person of Prince John—the whole presided over by a sick King, hag-ridden by conscience, dreaming of a Crusade to the Holy Land as M. Remorse thinks of slimming and repentance. Those who see the world of *Henry IV* as some vital, joyous Renaissance England must go behind the facts Shakespeare presents. It is a world where to be normal is to be anti-social, and to be social is to be anti-human. Humanity is split in two. One half is banished to an underworld where dignity and decency must inevitably submerge in brutality and riot. The other half is restricted to an over-world where the same dignity and decency succumb to heartlessness and frigidity.

We said at the outset that Hal is Shakespeare's consciousness, and Falstaff Shakespeare's unconscious, Hal the exhaustion of old meanings, Falstaff the sign of ultimate renewal. And this is a half-departure from the view put forward above that Hal and Falstaff are ideologically the same thing. It creates an ultimate difference between Hal and Falstaff, in terms of Shakespeare's development. The apparent inconsistency comes from a shift of viewpoint which I think it is necessary to make. We have fitted Falstaff into the conscious meanings of *Henry IV*. He is, however, more than this. He points towards the world of Shakespeare's tragedies—as we said, to Lear; as Bradley insists, to Hamlet and Cleopatra. Falstaff has a touch of infinity, Bradley rightly claims, which is denied to Hal. He is certainly big enough almost to wander away on his own and escape inclusion in any of the systematic history-schemes of Shakespeare's chronicle plays. He has a richness of raw human potential not found anywhere else in Shakespeare before 1600; he is a fund of matter capable of taking the impress of any form, a symbol of Shakespeare's fecundity itself. Pity, love, and fear are not ideally embodied in

Henry IV, not even in Falstaff. But pity and love Falstaff certainly attracts to himself. No-one quickens such loyal and selfless devotion as he does, nor in such unpromising material: in Bardolph, Nym, Pistol, Mistress Quickly, and poor Doll Tearsheet. Here in the underworld is strange seed beneath the snow.—And fear? For that we have to wait until Falstaff's death-bed ramblings in *Henry V*:

> Nay, sure hee's not in Hell: hee's in *Arthurs* Bosome, if ever man went to *Arthurs* Bosome: a made a finer end, and went away an it had beene any Christome Child: a parted ev'n just betweene Twelve and One, ev'n at the turning o' th' Tyde: for after I saw him fumble with the Sheets, and play with Flowers, and smile upon his fingers end, I knew there was but one way: for his Nose was as sharpe as a Pen, and a Table of greene fields. How now Sir *John* (quoth I) what man? be a good cheer: so a cryed out, God, God, God, three or foure times. . . .
>
> (*Henry V*, II, iii.)

Falstaff dying fumbles with the sheets as with his beads, and tries maybe to repeat the verses of the twenty-third Psalm about the 'green fields' and the 'table'. No audience doubts that Falstaff ends in Abraham's bosom. Is it by an unconscious echo of *King John* that Shakespeare calls it *Arthur's* bosom?

We can sum up now the relation in which the Prince Hal plays stand to the earlier tetralogy and to *King Lear*.

The earlier plays hold fast to a Christian belief in the primacy of 'pity, love, and fear'. Against this theological background is thrown the figure of the machiavel—not a melodramatic monster, but the interpreter of an actual society. The machiavel rejects 'pity, love, and fear' and kills the King who stands for the holy order of these values. The machiavel is a successful social man, an animal perfectly adjusted to the new realm of Commodity. Shakespeare in *Richard III*, however, is aware of the diabolism of the New Man. *King John* begins a process of accommodation to the New Man and the New World of Commodity. The rigid theological frame of God's revenges is abandoned. The absolute sphere of value is now the world of history—a world without 'pity, love, and fear' in which the task is now to fashion a hero in terms of the actual political world. The Bastard son of Coeur de Lion is Shakespeare's first sketch for this hero: a man of courage, strength, and unqualified patriotism; a New Man, too, however—up from the country, impudent, ambitious, machiavellian, a rationalist, an opportunist, and with no illusions: good human material for the 'tug and scamble' that is to come. An echo of the earlier theology is felt in *King John* in the Bastard's sense that his society is deplorable and sets deplorable conditions. It is a 'mad world, mad Kings, mad composition' but there is no alternative.

The Prince Hal plays bring this phase of Shakespeare's development to an end. Hal, Hotspur, Falstaff, the whole body of the play's world now reveals clearly the mechanisms of sixteenth century society. Commodity is both ruler and ruled. Authority and Appetite, combined and disjoined alternately, set up the swaying, skidding rhythm which 'tug and scamble' requires. Hal's descent is direct from Richard Crookback, through the Bastard in *King John*. The villain of the first tetralogy is transformed into the hero of the second. Hal is the machiavel of goodness. He is also the official side of Elizabeth's world, and as such stands for Authority. Companion to him first, then rejected by him, is Falstaff—the unofficial side of Elizabeth's world, boisterous vitality and blindly unscrupulous Appetite. There is no vestige in this world of 'pity, love, and fear', not even the awareness that 'pity, love, and fear' are dead. The theology of the plays is the no-theology of Tudor propaganda.

Henry IV is the culminating development of Shakespeare in the Histories. In terms of Shakespeare's fuller and continued development into the tragic phase *Henry IV* is obviously, of course, transitional. How transitional *King Lear* enables us to see. *Henry IV* is only immature when we compare Shakespeare with himself.

King Lear's synthesis resolves the false conflicts and false solutions of the later histories. It amounts to another turn of the screw, a further, and, I think, a final stage in Shakespeare's inner development. In some respects the development has the appearance of a return to the world-view of *Henry VI*. In *King Lear* Shakespeare again finds a means of putting the actual society of Power and Appetite in a wider frame. This frame embodies again the instinctive human standards of 'pity, love, and fear'. The machiavels still govern, but there is no attempt to whitewash them. Edmund carries on the virtues of Richard, Falconbridge, and Hal. Shakespeare is scrupulously fair to his qualities. He no longers pretends, however, that they are desirably exercised in the maintenance of an order which—for the very best of state reasons—can turn out Lear and blind Gloster. Shakespeare finds a means to condemn the society he knows is historically inevitable. Against it he holds up not only the ideal of a transcendent community, but also the needs of a real humanity to which the operations of actual society perpetually do violence: an idea of unqualified goodness which cannot be measured by success in a corrupt society, a goodness more inclusive than that covered by the governmental maxims of state-expediency. This new thing which Shakespeare discovers and asserts about man, society, and the universe is Cordelia.

CHAPTER II

THE FOOL AND HANDY-DANDY

———

I propose in this chapter to isolate one aspect of the Fool. The aim is to see how far Shakespeare's larger theme—the theme of man and his society, of the two Natures and Janus-like Reason—is reflected in the shivered mirror of the Fool's verse.

The manner of that verse is gnomic and elliptic. It is an ideal idiom for twisting broken fragments into unexpected patterns. On one side it might originate in the medieval nonsense poem. The sixteenth century popular ballad still kept this alive in such scraps and oddments as the Fool sings. On the other it comes down through Shakespeare's own period of Gobbo-like confusion-mongering. It ends, in *King Lear*, as the sort of thing Blake might have taken as a model for his own octosyllables. It is not a carefree or a happy verse, for all its capering and jauntiness. It is taut with anxiety and bafflement, with distress and bitterness. It is abrupt and bewildered. It can juggle with fragments of the two Natures and the two Reasons, and then shrug off the whole business with hideous flippancy. Pain distorts the Fool's grimace, but the pain might equally mask compassion or contempt.

A passage from the Fool's first scene in the play provides a fair example of his normal idiom:

LEAR: When were you wont to be so full of songs, sirrah?
FOOL: I have used it nuncle, e'er since thou mad'st thy daughters thy mothers, for when thou gav'st them the rod, and put'st down thy own breeches,

Then they for sudden joy did weep,
     And I for sorrow sung,
That such a King should play bo-peep,
     And go the fools among.
Prithee nuncle keep a schoolmaster that can teach
     thy fool to lie, I would fain learn to lie.
LEAR: An you lie, sirrah, we'll have you whipped.

(I, iv.)

We might note first that the Fool is under a compulsion to tell the truth, so that what he says has professional reliability. Second, the popular ballad material incorporated into his part is not chosen at random: it matches his own manner, and throws new light on what he has to say. Thirdly, very often his speeches deliberately re-state what has already been given expression in the play elsewhere. 'Thou mad'st thy daughters thy mothers', for example, repeats Goneril's outburst of the scene before:

          Idle old man
     That still would manage those authorities
     That he hath given away, now by my life,
     Old fools are babes again, and must be us'd
     With checks as flatteries, when they are seen abus'd.

(I, iii.)

Each of these points is a commonplace of criticism: their combined force is sufficient warrant for treating the whole of the Fool's lines as serious and homogeneous utterance. His statements have as much weight, for interpretation, as those of anyone in the play.

The most significant aspect of the Fool's verse is also illustrated in the passage. This is his habit of translating everything into handy-dandy. (Cp. 'When a man is over-lusty at legs, then he shall wear wooden nether-stocks.')

He sees everything as a see-saw. Whichever end of the see-saw anyone chooses, the Fool's job is to be counterweight. The King himself is an instance of this universal handy-dandy. He has made his daughters his mothers. Instead of wielding the rod, he receives correction himself. Instead of remaining a ruler on the throne he has become an irresponsible child playing bo-peep. Handy-dandy is a psychological law, too:

> Then they for sudden joy did weep
> And I for sorrow sung.

The ballad lines, apart from the *King Lear* context, are merely Launcelot Gobbo silliness. In the *King Lear* context, however, they develop characteristic overtones. There is first the obvious common-sense meaning: excessive joy can make one weep, and hysterical sorrow will sometimes sing. But this in itself shows how the mind rocks perpetually between extremes, with no fixed centre of measure or control. Furthermore there is the meaning that comes from the deliberate switching of the tears and the song. The daughters have stolen the Fool's tears; he is left to sing their song. It might be a profound hypocrisy on the daughters' part—the kind of hypocrisy that steals the good man's weapons and leaves him with none but those the hypo-crite has discarded. (This, of course, is Cordelia's plight when she must be dumb because the hypocrites have already made truth seem like a lie.) Hypocrisy can always seize the initiative, put truth in this false position and leave it paralysed and immobile; hypocrisy can force even truth to seem a collaborator. The Fool appears to be as callous as the sisters, they are no more cruel than he. The Fool can see it all happening, and knows exactly how it works. But his knowledge leaves him no better off. It is all an inevitable and miserable handy-dandy.

A striking thing about the Fool is that while his heart makes him belong to the Lear-party, and while his loyalty to Lear him-self is unshakeable, his head can only represent to him that mean-ing for Reason which belongs to the party of Edmund and the Sisters. He is aware of the two common senses in the debate be-tween Goneril and Albany. But his constant recommendation to the King and his following is a counsel of self-interest. Here is his advice to Kent:

Let go thy hold, when a great wheel runs down a hill, lest it breaks thy

neck with following. But the great one that goes upward, let him
draw thee after: when a wise man gves thee better council give me
mine again: I would have none but Knaves follow it since a Fool
gives it:

> That Sir, which serves and seeks for gain,
>   And follows but for form;
> Will pack, when it begins to rain,
>   And leave thee in the storm,
> But I will tarry, the Fool will stay,
>   And let the wise man fly:
> The Knave turns Fool that runs away,
>   The Fool no Knave perdy. (II, ii.)

It is usual to claim that in instances such as this the Fool is sub-
mitting the loyalty of Lear's following to a test. He gives advice
which he knows will not be taken by the disinterested; he is a
hypocrite in a benevolent sense. This view, I think, makes the
Fool less ambiguous than he really is. As I see him, he really does
believe that to follow Lear to disaster is foolishness. Absolute
loyalty is irrational, and the Fool never suggests that there is a
supernatural sanction for such irrationality. Folly is an alternative to knavery, certainly. But that does not make it a virtue.
The third term that would rescue him from the counter-
balancing negatives is simply missing. Handy-dandy works on
the ethical level, too. It is this which separates the Fool from
Albany whom Goneril calls a 'moral fool'. The Fool can see no
sense in the foolish morality Albany would urge his wife to
pursue. On the other hand, Goneril's alternative is no more
acceptable. The Fool is quite clear on the point that such common sense as hers (such wisdom) is mere knavishness. Wiseman has come to mean for him, as for Bunyan later, worldly-
wiseman. Unlike Bunyan the Fool does not see the wiseman as
a candidate for damnation.

Handy-dandy operates in society, too. The 'great wheel' runs
down the hill and another is drawn upward by its very descent.
It is tempting to see behind this image some new device of
haulage machinery. (Massinger's image for the great man and

his satellites was the great wheel of a mill that makes the lesser wheels go round. In Chapman the wheels are those of a spit.) The wheel is probably, however, the wheel of Fortune. Either way a strong sense pervades the lines of the individual's weakness in the authoritarian setting for human action. The Great Man himself is as insecure as the small man. The tilted plane of society makes tug and scamble inevitable. Under such conditions the panic of save-your-own-skin will be the prevailing mood.

The Fool holds up to Lear a model of cautionary excellence. It is the hypocrite, the canny capitalist, and the self-denying puritan combined:

> Mark it, nuncle;
> Have more than thou showest,
> Speak less than thou knowest,
> Lend less than thou owest,
> Ride more than thou goest,
> Learn more than thou trowest,
> Set less than thou throwest;
> Leave thy drink and thy whore,
> And keep in a door,
> And thou shalt have more,
> Than two tens to a score. (I, iv.)

Goneril has already charged Lear with the vices of the old regime, riotous 'Epicurism and Lust'—the excess of those impulses which, in the mean, are sociability, comradeship, free self-expression, and love. The Fool prescribes the complementary vices of the new dispensation: a riot of acquisitiveness, self-protection, suspicion.

Again, it is impossible to say that the advice is meant only as irony. The model proposed is certainly mean and contemptible, an inversion of the grand image of the King in the scheme of natural theology. It is not one that would be freely espoused if other alternatives were open. However, the Fool doubts whether any alternative does lie open, apart from the permanent alternative of Folly.

We are tempted to think of the Fool as being on the side of some social Utopia, until we see handy-dandy applied to this, too:

> When priests are more in word, than matter;
> When brewers mar their malt with water;
> When nobles are their tailors' tutors,
> No heretics burned, but wenches' suitors;
> When every case in Law, is right;
> No squire in debt, nor no poor knight;
> When slanders do not live in tongues;
> Nor cutpurses come not to throngs;
> When usurers tell their gold i' th' field,
> And bawds, and whores, do churches build,
> Then shall the Realm of Albion,
> Come to great confusion;
> Then comes the time, who lives to see't,
> That going shall be us'd with feet.
> This prophecy Merlin shall make, for I live before his
>   time.   (III, ii.)

The first four lines describe the actual state of present corruption. The next four switch without warning to the coming Utopia. The two lines following manage to mix both together:

> When usurers tell their gold i' th' field,
> And bawds, and whores, do churches build.

We can read this either as total conversion or as utter unregeneracy. The confusion is completed by the last four lines. The Golden Age to come will entail the overthrow of Albion, and the last stage will return us to the point from which we start:

> Then comes the time, who lives to see't,
> That going shall be us'd with feet.

There is little hope of enlisting the Fool as a social reformer.

Handy-dandy is even applied to Time: 'This prophecy', the Fool explains, 'Merlin shall make; for I live before his time'. Direction and purpose in history itself are lost. The motion from past to future becomes that of a wheel again.

The wheel is the key to much of the Fool's imagery. The great wheel running up and down the hill is a double wheel-image—a wheel running round in a circle. We used the image of the see-saw to explain the working of the Fool's opposites. A suspended wheel is an endless series of see-saws. The old man and the babe, the moralist and the knave, the wise man and the fool—these are opposites diametrically counterpoised, and then (since the wheel always comes full circle) identified. The mechanism is shown at work in the individual, in society, in the pattern of the moral world, and in history itself. Man is caught in a contraption that bears him up and down, carries him round and round, continually.

Edmund and the Sisters see society as a competition; and Goneril says it is safer to fear than to trust too far. In this competitiveness there is a certain combative courage, and for them fear is an offensive-defensive of caution. Man even as an animal still retains a kind of dignity. He is King of the Beasts. The Fool sees this competitiveness and fear in a different light. 'He that has a house to put's head in', he remarks, 'has a good head-piece.' Or, another occasion:

FOOL: Canst tell why an oyster makes his shell?
LEAR: No.
FOOL: Nor I neither; but I can tell why a snail has a house.
LEAR: Why?
FOOL: Why, to put's head in, not to give it away to his daughters and leave his horns without a case.

(I, v.)

Here he makes the fear, timidity, and the creatures nearest to man in this general respect the close oyster and the fearful snail. Self-interest does not only lead to an aggressive outgoing among one's fellows. It leads also to a self-protective shrinkage within one's shell. Man is a poor, cowering, threatened creature, and will do well to look after himself as best he can.

The shell and the sheltering creature symbolize for the Fool man in the carapace of his society. The compelling factor in the image is the suggestion of the external threat. Man must defend himself in such an environment. His mean shifts are a necessity imposed on him by the sub-humanity of the surrounding universe, a universe constantly threatening to crush the shell men have built for themselves. It is this same sub-humanity (sensed by Kent, as well as by the Fool, as lying behind the Thunder) which amply sanctions man's inhumanity to man. Not all can be equally warm or sheltered. Those like Poor Tom who are pushed outside must blame themselves only—and the elements.

The Fool, like Hobbes, knows that 'the passion to be reckoned upon is fear'. Fear throbs as a motive through his human world, and beats down from the non-human world of the heavens. It is this underlying feeling which explains the Fool's sincerest piece of advice to the suffering King he accompanies over the heath. It is an example of compassion working to the same effect as cruelty: an unconscious handy-dandy. He is alone with Lear on the heath; the storm is still raging; the King has just called on the 'all-shaking thunder' to

> Strike flat the thick rotundity o' th' world,
> Crack Nature's moulds, all germens spill at once
> That makes ingrateful man. (III, ii.)

The Fool says:

> O nuncle, Court holy-water in a dry house, is better than this rain-water out o' door. Good nuncle, in, ask thy daughter's blessing; here's a night pities neither wise men, nor fools. (III, iii.)

The heath tests the breaking-points of the human beings wandering over it. This is the Fool's, and a nadir of negated humanity is reached. 'Court holy water' is the sycophancy and corruption of the time-servers that fawn on power. Under the threat of Thunder the Fool's opposition collapses. He will abjectly consent even to playing the hypocritical knave. He urges the king to accept the worst terms society can offer, the blessing of pelican daughters:

> The Knave turns Fool that runs away.

This is an ultimate bankruptcy. And it is the intellect's sincere advice. There is neither bitterness nor irony, only moral panic. We are invited back with Lear into the corrupt world we were glad to have quitted—invited to stand by the same fire with Lady Brach, and stink.

The corrupt world is the final clue to the meaning of the Fool. He is not of tragic scope. He affirms the dignity of man neither as animal nor angelic reason. Nor has he the ennobling weakness of compassion. He remains a figure of pathos because he is so helpless—helplessly immobilized by a handy-dandy of opposites neither of which he can choose. Nor will he admit of any third ground, the possibility that knavishness might not be an ultimate, that wisdom might be redeemable, that society might be capable of re-birth. He does not survive his own grim laughter, and disappears for that reason. He could not survive, without metamorphosis, in the same context as Cordelia. He is fast in the sickening stasis of his handy-dandy.

His summary of the human situation is as follows:

> He that has a house to put's head in, has a good head-piece:
> > The codpiece that will house,
> > Before the head has any;
> > The head, and he shall louse:
> > So beggars marry many.
> > The man that makes his toe,
> > What he his heart should make,
> > Shall of a corn cry woe,
> > And turn his sleep to wake.
> For there never yet was fair woman, but she made mouths in a glass.
>
> (III, ii.)

This is the closest knot Shakespeare ties in the idiom he invented for the Fool, and is original for both manner and matter.

That the imagery should be both social and sexual is not chance prurience. The idea of sexual love in Shakespeare's time was approaching the end of an interesting career. It had been a relation under which to figure the ideal destiny of man, both as a person and a social agent. In Spenser, for example, love is the consummation of the whole course of virtue in man. It may be that wherever love is more than casual mating it inevitably serves as an allegory of the marriage of the individual to truth. Throughout the Elizabethan period (and in Petrarch and Dante) this liaison seems certainly to have been well established. By 1600 optimism had reached its term (maybe a nemesis for Elizabeth's over-stimulation of the cult of Gloriana). In the Shakespearean breakdown of confidence, extending to most of the human values, love was also involved. *King Lear* reflects moods that are not only anti-authoritarian, and anti-social, but also anti-sexual. Love is left with none of the Spenserian glamour (except in relation to Cordelia) and the revulsion is expressed crudely—as by Lear in his mad speeches, and by the Fool here.

The codpiece is part of the gallant's costume, and also, quite simply, the phallus. The first four lines thus describe how improvident lechering leads to disease, and how this begins a vicious circle: because the head too (shrewd prudence and cautious provision against all the potential threats of life) becomes lousy. Once the process has started it is increasingly difficult to stop it. This is the explanation of the paradox concerning the Beggarman and his long train of doxies. He 'marries' so many because he is poor (the result of an initial imprudence), and not vice versa. The four lines give a kind of condensed Rake's Progress, and the career of proud gallant becoming Abram man conforms to the mechanism of the wheel. This central idea in the lines is repeated, of course, in Poor Tom—the courtier whose vices had just been those that set the wheel turning and who becomes a naked Bedlamite.

The next four lines fuse the images of Beggarman and Courtier after another fashion. The 'toe' can belong to either: it might be the Courtier's pinched in his over-tight shoes, or the Beggarman's that has burst through his boot. A sexual symbolism, paralleling 'codpiece', accompanies the social reference. The toe is also (*pace* Freud) the phallus.—I take the lines to mean: 'The man—rich or poor—who makes his 'toe' the centre of all his hopes, aspirations, and satisfactions, sacrificing, if he be a courtier, all real human feeling to vanity, or, if he be a beggar, squandering his emotional means in slovenly lust—this man, the composite social creature, will suffer the inevitable pain consequent on his perversity: pangs of guilty remorse that will never let him rest. Thus both extremes in society, acting in opposite ways from opposite motives, come together in the same state— a state of self-torment.'

Handy-dandy is doubly exerted in these lines. First, one half of society is neatly folded over the other. The quatrains seem at first sight to be referring only to one, but are in fact applicable to the other, too. The effect is to argue, seemingly, that haves and have-nots are in an identical plight. Secondly, through the intertwining of the social and sexual in the same image, the public world of community and the private world of personal emotional life are shown to interlock.

Yet a third handy-dandy remains to be noted. The poem is about the strife between head and heart, both of them sinning and sinned against. The first quatrain illustrates a sin against the head: lust flouts prudence, and the unregulated instinct after one's kind leads to disaster. The second depicts a sin against the heart: either by the vain courtier (cultivating the externals instead of attending to the inward things of the spirit) or through the coney-catching beggarman (exposing and parading his ill-shodness, yet not revealing the design and deceit in his breast). Head and heart, like courtier and beggarman are equally badly off. Neither is a reliable guide. Both are mutually confounding. The eight lines summarize the plight of a fissured society and of a divided man: a severance that is self-perpetuating and self-aggravating. Society and man come together only to make each other worse. This applies to rich as well as poor. At either end of the social scale (and it is a scale with no middle) we see a travesty of human nature—flaunting codpiece, calloused toe, man lacerated in head and heart, in mind and body, by disease or conscience.

To sum up, the Fool can be regarded as the consciousness of a split society. Like man, its creator, the society is a twin-headed monster at strife with itself. The Fool consistently uses the imagery of disease and perversity. Complementary ill-healths counterbalance in perpetual handy-dandy. He sees rich man and poor man, head and heart, sympathizes with neither, yet cannot dissociate himself from the conditions of the strife. Harsh as the handy-dandy world of corrupt society is, there is no escape from it: 'In, nuncle, in, and ask thy daughters' blessing.'

We began by observing the unconscious handy-dandy in the Fool's own behaviour. His head thinks with the Reason of Goneril and Regan, yet what he does is directly counter to the self-interest which for them and for him is the only thing that makes sense. His greatest bit of cruelty is wrung from him by compassion. While he counsels flight, with wiseman and knave, he will not desert the king: because he is a Fool. What he does will not square with what he says, and it is a redeeming insincerity. Wilfully and blindly he holds to the Great Wheel going downhill.

The Fool, I think, stands for the unillumined head—the intellect—as Lear is the soul, and Cordelia the spirit. He can discern in his cold light the alternatives between which he cannot choose. The sort of thing he could desire he will not admit to exist. It would be too good to be true. Nature in him is an arrest of motion. His head will not allow him to descend the scale with Edmund and the Sisters, and yet it shows no sign of rushing into the natural theology of Lear and Cordelia. The Fool is incapable of Goneril's wickedness, of Lear's error and his subsequent growth, of Cordelia's faultless integration. He prefers, however, to walk in a darkness he cannot fathom rather than stay in the light of such reason as he cannot abide. The head would betray him back to Goneril's hearth, with Lady Brach. But for reasons neither he nor the head knows he follows Lear over the heath.

CHAPTER III

CORDELIA

───────────

[a]

CORDELIA AND SHAKESPEARE CRITICISM

To understand Cordelia is to understand the whole play. It is a pity, therefore, that Cordelia should have been so unfortunate in her critics.

The trouble starts with the first scene. King Lear and his daughter are in a reciprocal relation. The misunderstanding of one leads to the misunderstanding of the other. The first scene, unhappily, is an interpretative crux. It has lead to the misunderstanding of both.

Before treating Cordelia as she is in the play I propose to treat her as she has appeared (in close connection with her father) in criticism. It is only so that the issues involved will become clear.

Dr. Johnson could not bear the ending of Shakespeare's *King Lear*. Part of his extreme sensitiveness might be due to the effect Cordelia had upon him. It was intolerable to the moral optimism of the eighteenth century that such transcendent goodness should not be taken care of in the human universe. The ending of the play was too painful for art. Dr. Johnson assented to the kindly impulse behind the version of Nahum Tate.

Coleridge is the grand original of the reading of Lear and Cordelia's conduct in the first scene which has become basic for

114

the canon. Coleridge comments on Cordelia's crucial reply as
follows:

There is something of disgust at the ruthless hypocrisy of her sisters,
and some little faulty admixture of pride and sullenness in Cordelia's
'Nothing'; and her tone is well contrived, indeed, to lessen the glaring
absurdity of Lear's conduct, but answers the yet more important
purpose of forcing away the attention from the nursery-tale, the
moment it has served its end, that of supplying the canvas for the
picture.

The theory of Cordelia's 'faulty admixture of pride' thus enters
the canon.

Coleridge's German contemporary, A. W. Schlegel, makes
no mention of the fault which Swinburne later says 'rescues
Cordelia from perfection'. Schlegel is prevented from seeing
any fault, as Dr. Johnson might have been:

Of Cordelia's heavenly beauty of soul, painted in so few words,
I will not venture to speak; she can only be named in the same breath
as Antigone.

Ulrici, however, whose handling of the play is brilliantly
Hegelian, takes up the Coleridgean hint and expands it:

Cordelia pays the penalty of the fault she committed, when, instead
of affectionately humouring the weakness of her aged father, she met
him with unfilial forwardness, and answered his, no doubt, foolish
questions with unbecoming harshness, and asperity; a father's curse
lights upon her head, and its direful consequences cannot afterwards
be avoided. The slighter her failing may appear, the deeper is the tragic
effect of its heavy penalty.

The wheel has come full circle. The death which Johnson had
thought 'contrary to the natural ideas of justice, to the hope
of the reader, and . . . to the faith of the chronicles' is now seen
as a stroke of profound philosophic insight: insight into the infallible retributory justice of the universe.

And so the stream springing from Coleridge might be followed: until (with Dr. J. Bucknill) Lear is stated to be already a

clinical case when the play opens, and Cordelia, therefore, stupid as well as proud. By way of complement to these nineteenth century comments we might turn to a mid-sixteenth century treatment of the duties children owe to parents. The following is from *The Catechism*, expounded by Thomas Becon, Cranmer's chaplain and Prebendary of Canterbury:

The honour and obedience is great, I confess, which the children owe to their parents: notwithstanding, if they command anything contrary to the word of God, in this behalf they are not to be obeyed. The honour due unto parents is so far to be executed, as it may stand with the honour of God. If it doth in any point obscure that, then it is utterly to be rejected and cast away. And we may right well and with a good conscience say: 'We must obey God rather than men.'

Becon says, in effect, that parents must first be sensible before filial obedience can be expected at all. The duty is not all on the children's side.

Finally we might listen to a Shakespearean comment on this first scene. The psychology is expert and Elizabethan. The speakers are cool rationalists when they look at human nature. Above all, they are in a position to know what they are talking about:

GONERIL: You see how full of changes his age is, the observation we have made of it hath (not?) been little; he always lov'd our sister most, and with what poor judgement he hath now cast her off, appears too grossly.

REGAN: 'Tis the infirmity of his age, yet he hath ever but slenderly known himself.

GONERIL: The best and soundest of his time hath been but rash, then must we look from his age to receive not alone the imperfections of long-ingraffed condition, but therewithal the unruly waywardness, that infirm and choleric years bring with them.

REGAN: Such inconstant starts are we like to have from him as this of Kent's banishment.

(I, i.)

Goneril and Regan can be assumed to be unbiased. It is to be

noted that their comment on the first scene makes no mention
of the old man's being already mad, nor of the partition being
a trick. Concerning Cordelia they preserve complete silence.
Neither her pride, sullenness, obstinacy, nor lack of human
judgment are referred to. Nothing, it would appear, needs to be
said. The father is a man of long-engraffed weak judgment; he is
rash at the best of times; now, choler working more freely on
the infirm spirits of extreme age, he is more than ever unstable.
Cordelia is his favourite daughter. Her virtues join with her
father's faults and her sisters' wickedness to make her 'Nothing'
both inevitable and right. Folk-tale is swift and unambiguous in
its initial moral distinctions. And once made the distinctions
of folk-tale are never revoked. The play in this first scene relies
on the folk-tale.

Like Edmund, Cordelia is not a complex character. With her,
as with Edmund, the main difficulty is to decide what exact
weight must be given to her in the general scheme of the play.
As with Edmund, so again with Cordelia, this involves more
than character-study. Cordelia is a compelling picture of a
young girl—as compelling in her way as Chaucer's Griselde is,
and similar in conception. Griselde is not only a character-
study, however: she stands in the framework of medieval
allegory and acquires meanings that transcend psychology.
Cordelia, I think, is a similar case.

The perspective in which psychology must be placed, if Cordelia is to be seen right, can be more readily appreciated if we
put Cordelia alongside another figure in literature who lived
through a scene with his father almost an exact repetition of the
scene between Cordelia and Lear. This is Blake's *A Little Boy
Lost*. The poem deserves to be quoted in full:

> 'Nought loves another as itself,
> Nor venerates another so,
> Nor is it possible to thought
> A greater than itself to know:

'And, Father, how can I love you
Or any of my brothers more?
I love you like the little bird
That picks up crumbs around the door.'

The Priest sat by and heard the child,
In trembling zeal he seiz'd his hair:
He led him by his little coat,
And all admir'd the priestly care.

And standing on the altar high,
'Lo! what a fiend is here', said he,
'One who sets reason up for judge
Of our most holy Mystery?'

The weeping child could not be heard,
The weeping parents wept in vain;
They stripp'd him to his little shirt,
And bound him in an iron chain;

And burn'd him in a holy place,
Where many had been burn'd before:
The weeping parents wept in vain.
Are such things done on Albion's shore?

We can imagine the father to have just finished speaking
when the poem opens. The question the Little Boy answers in
the first two verses must have been very similar to that addressed
by Lear to his daughters. It is the common enough question:
'Whom do you love best in all the world?' Like Lear, the Father
makes himself the sole judge of moral worth. The answer he
wants, of course, is the hypocritical one usual to such occasions.
The Little Boy must say that he loves his father and his brothers
best. This will prove him to be unselfish, and his unselfishnesss
prove him to be good. Unfortunately, the Little Boy says the
wrong thing. He says the wrong thing from the Father's point
of view, but the reader of the poem is to know from the outset
that the Little Boy is sensible, good, and honest: it is the Father
who is mistaken. The Little Boy's,

Nought loves another as itself,

goes back to Rousseau's *amour de soi*. It is also common sense, and as a law of Nature discoverable by the Light of Reason it goes back beyond Rousseau, through Hooker, to the Middle Ages. Dante's *Convivio* (and the same is in Chaucer) makes proper self-love integral to the true love of God and one's neighbour.

Already it is quite obvious that Blake is doing more than drawing a naturalistic sketch of a domestic scene—though the naturalis: in the first verses is also indubitable. The Little Boy's words place the whole poem in a context of thought and moral discussion. By so doing they make the Little Boy a portent rather than a character. Even the two lines that follow the first are a particular allusion:

> Nor is it possible to thought
> A greater than itself to know,

—this is the Little Boy's English version of *cogito ergo sum*. The Father is convicted of silliness and unreasonableness: he neither knows himself, the nature of things, nor his son. The second verse gives the rebuke with just the right amount of mild—almost tender—surprise. It gives us the measure of the full instinctive integrity of the Little Boy in his innocence, and makes furt' nore the dainty observation that all creatures belong to themsaves and to all others:

> I love you like the little bird
> That picks up crumbs around the door.

The proper kind of unselfishness is merely sharing the over-plus of our proper selfishness.

The Priest in the poem recalls Voltaire and Tom Paine, but along with Reason and Holy Mystery he is likely to go back, too, in Blake's case, through the 'obscure nonconformity' in which Blake was brought up, to the jibes of Cromwell's sectaries. For Gerrard Winstanley as for Blake the Priest and the

King both had a vested interest in Holy Mystery. The truth, on the other hand, was plain and open to Reason and as common to man as daylight: love God and your neighbour as yourself, forbear to be oppressive, cruel, or covetous, and dig the common land. From his nearness to the Priest, and still following the late-seventeenth-century nonconformist tradition, the Father in Blake's poem is obviously also the Magistrate.

Thus Father, Priest, and King are all merged in the single combine that rejects the Little Boy's wisdom and finally burns him at the stake. Towards the end of the poem, when the tragedy is being pushed to a conclusion, when it is out of the hands of people and in the hands of officials, common humanity asserts itself in the parents in spite of their indoctrination. But the parents' tears are vain. Their foolishness has started something it cannot stop. Blake's poem ends with that sudden turn of the head which is characteristic of his poetry:

> Are such things done on Albion's shore?

The story is an allegory, and the allegory refers to current practice. Behind the poem is the time.

In *A Little Boy Lost* Blake is interested in weighing and re-estimating the whole morality of unselfishness. Naturally this cannot be discussed apart from the questions of what happens when real people do this rather than that. The issue can be stated, however, without any particularity of character or circumstance.

Shakespeare's first scene in *King Lear* puts forward a situation of a similar type, with, I think, a precisely similar emphasis. Shakespeare is evaluating alternative shapings of conduct, the alternative natures of the parties involved, Edmund and the Sisters on one side, and Cordelia on the other. The traditional morality is weighed against the morality of the New Man. As befits a drama, there is more detailed concern with character and circumstance than there is in Blake's poem. But the order of importances is the same: the characters are there to express the natures, and not the natures the characters. It is how they stand with regard to Nature that gives each character whatever importance it carries in the play.

Cordelia, then, has been served very badly by the criticism that has gone to Shakespeare's plays solely as a quarry for character studies. This same criticism is that which, basing itself on nineteenth-century practice, has hailed character-portrayal as the be-all and end-all in both the drama and the novel. It is responsible for imposing alien standards on the work of earlier times. It has upset the traditional relationships between the various kinds of meaning a literary work can have.

Shakespeare is undeniably a great portrayer of character, a subtle and no doubt conscious investigator of motive. He is moving towards character study as the nineteenth-century novelist might conceive it. At the same time he writes in a convention not tied to the precise and limiting rules observed by naturalism. He does not operate on the assumption that story is explicable as what people do, and that what people do is a result of what people are, and that what people are can be exhibited by displaying fully their motives, and that these motives are a product of heredity and environment. These are the literary habits of the nineteenth century. They imply, themselves, a philosophy of man. Character in the nineteenth century (as Bradley is led to say it is in Shakespeare)—Character is Fate.

Shakespeare was moving towards character-study. His conventions did not limit him, however, to an interest in character only. Nor, in portraying character, was he restricted to one clear and rigid method. In addition, he is a contemporary of Spenser, and stands closer than we do to the Morality. The people of his stories can have a direct relation to ideas behind the story (as they can in Spenser), and story, finally, can exist independently for its own sake: and it, too, can have direct access to the body of meaning that informs it. Shakespeare, that is, has not utterly left behind him the mental habits and the artistic attitudes of the Middle Ages. It can be said, at least, that he stands nearer to Malory than he does to Thackeray, nearer to Chaucer than to Galsworthy. And for the Middle Ages allegory-hunting was as exciting as motive-hunting is for us.

Modern criticism has become interested again in what it calls 'the different levels of meaning' in a literary work. It is sometimes hazy and confused when it operates with the notion. But already the change in approach has set Shakespeare free from the more obvious mis-handlings.

The Middle Ages had its own theory of 'the different levels of meaning'. They were defined with the kind of exactness we have not yet found either possible or necessary. Of the *Divine Comedy* Dante wrote:

. . . this work is not simple, but may rather be called polysemous, that is of many senses. For the sense that is gathered by the letter is one, and the sense that is gathered by the things signified by the letter another; and the first is called literal, but the second allegorical or mystical.

These allegorical meanings are themselves further subdivided into three.

Dante's four meanings are the same as those provided to guide the medieval homilist by Master Ripon of Durham in a conscientious early fifteenth-century account. The first degree is the literal or historical sense: this is what the words seem to say on a first glance. Then comes the allegorical sense, 'when one thing is said and another thing is understood by it' —for example, Abraham's two sons by his wife and his maid-servant signify the two Testaments. The third is the tropological or moral: this emerges when some general application can be made of either the literal or the allegorical senses. Finally there is the anagogical sense, when a scripture expounded in any of the three foregoing senses is further applied so that it 'signifies again some portion of the supernal things of eternal glory'.

Shakespeare stood closer to the allegorizing Middle Ages than we do now. The second edition of Sir John Harington's *Orlando Furioso* appeared in 1607 with a commentary on each book still following the medieval interpretative scheme: only the 'anagogical' section was omitted (presumably because Ariosto was profane) and in its place a section included on 'Allusions'.

But the argument for Shakespeare's thinking of his art in ways nearer to the medieval habits does not have to base itself on the rash assumption that the medieval habits as such were still operative, at however far a remove. It is sounder to claim (with Dr. Richards as well as with Dante) that 'levels of meaning' are inescapable in literature, because they point to a way in which the mind works, and because they indicate something permanent in its structure. The interpretative scheme of the Middle Ages is one which every age revises but never altogether rejects. Not even the nineteenth century could escape it.

From Coleridge to Bradley critics could not help going much further beyond character-study proper than they thought. For Coleridge, Shakespeare was the most philosophical of poets. We have made the point that even the character-approach to Shakespeare implies a philosophy of man and his place in the universe. In the mid-nineteenth-century criticism of Ulrici this is more than apparent:

... with what correctness and verisimilitude the several personages are made to work upon and modify each other, so as to throw out and illustrate their several characters, and at the same time bring about this particular course of tragic development: to recognize and estimate aright all these poetical excellences is an easy task for a generally well-educated man of these days. But to understand the organic coherence of the whole—to discover the intrinsic necessity of the tragic development in all its moments—to find the fundamental idea—the living centre, as it were, around which the several parts revolve, and thereby adjust themselves into a whole—all this requires profundity of view and a firm aesthetical basis of criticism.

Ulrici's Hegelian search for the 'fundamental idea', the 'living centre, as it were, around which the several parts revolve', is strictly equivalent to the medieval search for the anagogical explanation: the last and final meaning that can be wrung from anything. Modern criticism in its search for central themes is merely going back beyond its immediate forerunners who were most excited over psychology. At its worst, and against Dante's advice, it tends to start its building with the top storey.

Shakespeare's work, then, on any view, has 'different levels of meaning'. The weighing of one morality against another, which is the fundamental intention of *King Lear* as it is of Blake's *A Little Boy Lost*, I regard as an act of anagogical scope. The play opens with a demand that we should examine again our habitual approvals. At the end we might be returned to the same approvals. In the meantime, however, they will have been submitted to a deepening and re-invigorating inspection. At the end freshness will have been reunited to familiarity.

In all Shakespeare's work character as such must be subordinated to the 'idea' which ensures 'the organic coherence of the whole'. This idea, in *King Lear*, is the idea of Nature.

The implications of Edmund's Goddess led through contemporary thought into contemporary life. From the abstraction we were driven to the reality of a character. Behind the character stood an order of historical actuality to which Shakespeare had finally orientated himself.

Cordelia impresses us right from the outset as a character 'of unmingled tenderness and strength'. She is also, and immediately, related to the anagogical intention of the scene. She is, Lear says,

> a wretch whom Nature is ashamed
> Almost t'acknowledge hers. (I, i.)

'She is herself a dowry', France counters:

> Fairest Cordelia, that art most rich being poor,
> Most choice forsaken, and most lov'd despis'd,
> Thee and thy virtues here I seize upon,
> Be it lawful I take up what's cast away. (I, i.)

Cordelia is the other Nature Edmund, Goneril, and Regan

ignore. In our view she is a figure comparable with that of Griselde or Beatrice: literally a woman; allegorically the root of individual and social sanity; tropologically Charity 'that suffereth long and is kind'; anagogically the redemptive principle itself. The Gentleman in Act IV, vi, says of Lear:

> Thou hast a daughter
> Who redeems Nature from the general curse
> Which twain have brought her to.

The twain referred to are not Goneril and Regan. Quite obviously Shakespeare is referring here to Adam and Eve.

It is this Cordelia we must now proceed to examine.

[b]

CORDELIA AS NATURE

The argument in this section, is then, that Cordelia embodies the Nature which Edmund denies to exist, and which Lear—although he believes in it—cannot recognize when it is before him. By this we shall mean that Cordelia does not cease to be a woman, since the Nature she stands for is essentially human and requires incarnation. We shall try to show that this normative humanity embodied in Cordelia incorporates the traditional ideals of 'natural theology'; and that, furthermore, this ideal requires not only perfection in the individual, but perfection in the community also. In other words, Cordelia cannot stand for individual sanity without at the same time standing for rightness in the relation of man to man—social sanity. In so far as there is always a discrepancy between the truth the person aims at and the actual setting which makes it necessary to have that truth for an aim—in so far as the good man is necessarily in relation to a bad society—the ideal community Cordelia implies will be a non-existent one. If we like we can call it a Utopia. If we like we can call it, as the evangelicals and the apocalyptics did, Jerusalem. Art, like ethical action, is utopian in intention. Cordelia expresses the utopian intention of Shakespeare's art.

This last point is of some importance. What is at stake is the real reference which Shakespeare's art makes to Shakespeare's times, through its being the utterance of a historical person. The nineteenth century postponed the question of this reference by its notion of 'impersonal genius'. Even now criticism is loth to claim anything for Shakespeare the man on the mere strength of what it knows about Shakespeare the dramatist. It follows that everything Shakespeare says is credited with 'dramatic truth' only. As such, it is explained away. But Shakespeare, I think, was interested in other truths beside the 'dramatic'. I feel certain that *King Lear* is not more impersonal than the Sonnets are. And the Sonnets are not all or not merely formal 'dramatic' exercises.

Cordelia is a combination of gentleness and toughness. This combination represents something in the grain of Shakespeare's own nature, too. We think of him in his tragic period as a tough-minded man. His contemporaries, however, always spoke of him as 'gentle'. Both the gentleness and the toughness, in Cordelia and in Shakespeare, belong together. They are aspects of the same thing. What this is we can only describe as an eminent degree of 'integration': the reconciliation of passion with order, of impulse and law, of duty and desire. It is the romantic 'wholeness' Coleridge ascribes to Dorothy, and Wordsworth depicts in Lucy:

> Myself will to my darling be
> Both law and impulse; and with me
> The Girl, in rock and plain,
> In earth and heaven, in glade and bower,
> Shall feel an overseeing power
> To kindle and restrain.

Cordelia, for Shakespeare, is virtue. Like Wordsworth's Lucy, she stands for wholeness. Shakespeare conceives this integration, of course, after the manner of the traditional morality. More important still (and still within the general tradition of renaissance poetic theory) Shakespeare thinks of his art as having the celebration and definition of this virtue for its aim. The most relevant comment on *King Lear* in this respect is that of the *Sonnets*:

> Tir'd with all these, for restful death I cry:
> As to behold desert a beggar born,
> And needy nothing trimm'd in jollity,
> And purest faith unhappily forsworn,
> And gilded honour shamefully misplac'd,
> And maiden virtue rudely strumpeted,
> And right perfection wrongfully disgrac'd,
> And strength by limping sway disabled,
> And art made tongue-tied by authority,
> And folly doctor-like controlling skill,
> And simple truth miscall'd simplicity,
> And captive good attending captain ill:
> Tir'd with all these, from these would I be gone,
> Save that, to die, I leave my love alone.

The Cordelia-like toughness and tenderness are strongly in evidence here. The sonnet deals with virtue in its frustrating social environment. Shakespeare lists the wrenchings away of humanity from the frame of Nature. Along with the warping of virtue goes the parallel monstrosity:

> . . . art made tongue-tied by authority.

What Blake will later call 'Empire' exerts its counter-pressure against the wholeness which 'Art' must express, against the virtue it must champion. The utopian intention of art, and the inevitable political reaction to this intention, could not be made more explicit.

In the sonnet the poet confronts his own immediate world in his own particular person. The components of that world are familiar enough: the noble soul born a beggar; the penniless spendthrift going in for social ostentation; nonentities shamelessly advanced to eminent positions; the natively intelligent forced to carry out the executive instructions of the feeble minded but influential; dramatists submitted to the censorship of politicians; idiots doctoring and directing the labours of the skilful; simple truth called simple mindedness; goodness in chains and wickedness its gaoler—Shakespeare says nothing he does not also say or imply in *King Lear*. So we are entitled to claim for the play the same literal references to 'the times' we can claim for the sonnet. Cordelia is only a figure in his drama after she has been a discovery in Shakespeare's own consciousness. And she is not only Nature—the Nature violated in society. She is also Art—the Art pledged to present and express the wholeness society violates. Cordelia is the apex of Shakespeare's mind.

A hundred years' tradition has found fault with Cordelia's action in the first scene. In the hands of critics since Coleridge she has been

> Simple truth miscall'd simplicity.

The line from the sonnet could serve as the text for her rehabilitation.

The source of the accusation of 'pride' is of course Lear himself, the first person to insist that Cordelia was wrong: 'Let pride', he says,

> Let pride, which she calls plainness, marry her.   (I, i.)

But Shakespeare did not intend Lear to be taken as an infallible judge. Everyone around him knows he is committing an elementary mistake. Twenty lines later Kent picks up the word 'plainness' and reapplies it favourably:

> . . . be Kent unmannerly,
> When Lear is mad, what wouldst thou do old man?
> Think'st thou that duty should have leave to speak,
> When power to flattery bows? To plainness honour's bound,
> When Majesty falls to folly.   (I, i.)

In replying, Lear hurls the accusation of 'pride' at Kent, too, for his interference:

. . . thou hast sought to make us break our vows,
Which we durst never yet; and with strain'd pride,
To come betwixt our sentence, and our power,
Which, nor our nature, nor our place can bear.   (I, i.)

As a matter of common sense the virtue that feeds a sense of
pride is one thing, the proper obdurateness of virtue standing its
ground against hypocrisy and wrongheadedness is another. Cordelia had either to quail before Lear's rage, make goodness pay
homage to hypocrisy, or act as she does. With complete courage,
complete clear-headedness and implicit confidence both in herself and in the 'simple truth', she holds out against her father and
stands apart from her sisters. In this first scene her toughness is
indistinguishable from her gentleness.

With deliberate accuracy and under-emphasis she grounds her
conduct on the Law of Nature; that system of rightnesses in
human relations which from one standpoint are seen as duties,
from another as the fulfilment of normal instincts:

I love your Majesty
According to my bond, no more nor less.   (I, i.)

For Cordelia 'bond' means 'natural tie', a duty willingly accepted and gladly carried out because it answers to right instinct.
For Lear, however, as for the critics after Johnson, 'bond' rings
with a dead note. Shakespeare himself, of course, might have
unwittingly contributed to a sinister interpretation of the word.
He made Shylock a stickler for his 'bond'. From the standpoint
of the Renaissance prince, too, a 'bond' was not always a holy
or a binding thing. Entered into during a period of financial
stress, a 'bond' could be an obligation to pay which the Prince
gladly dishonoured, when possible, by invoking the medieval
law of nature and usury. For both the sixteenth century and for
the romantics, therefore, a 'bond' is a potentially frigid thing.
For the Middle Ages and for Cordelia, on the other hand, the
word means: 'I love you as every normal girl loves her father—
naturally!' Because of its double of meaning the word 'bond'

presents the two sides of the debate at once: on the one hand the inclusive scheme of natural law which Kings as well as ploughboys can violate; on the other, the absolute claim to full and total obedience. Where Blake in his poem had to define the Little Boy's position by three or four philosophical announcements, Shakespeare could rely on the transit of meanings taking place inside a single word.

Lear has a momentary hesitation. It is as if he himself were caught in transit between the two meanings:

> How now Cordelia? Mend your speech a little,
> Lest you may mar your Fortunes.   (I, i.)

In complying Cordelia expounds the obvious. Her speech sounds plain and stiff, almost clumsy. But the stiffness is neither priggish nor condescending. It is the sudden awkwardness of anyone who has assumed the self-evidence of the obvious, and is still called on to say what she means:

> Good my Lord,
> You have begot me, bred me, lov'd me. I
> Return those duties back as are right fit,
> Obey you, love you, and most honour you.
> Why have my sisters husbands, if they say
> They love you all? Happily when I shall wed,
> That Lord, whose hand must take my plight, shall carry
> Half my love with him, half my care, and duty,
> Since I shall never marry like my sisters
> To love my father all.   (I, i.)

The situation could not be made plainer to an audience aware of *The Forme of Solemnizacion of Matrimonie*:

> Wilt thou obey him, and serve him, love, honor, and kepe him in sickness and in health? And forsaking al other kepe thee only to him.

Cordelia's 'Obey you, love you, . . . honour you' alludes to the marriage vow, which she devastatingly reminds her married sisters of in the lines immediately following. Lear should be the first to appreciate her point. Cordelia's suitors are waiting out-side. Her share of the Kingdom is also intended to be a dowry. But Cordelia's exposition of the unambiguous Prayer Book is as lost on Lear as her use of the ambiguous 'bond'. Lear has fallen from the bias of Nature. He is dead to the meanings of the traditional morality.

The idea that Cordelia is proud has grown up as a result of the dissolution of the notion of 'Nature' as understood in the Middle Ages and in the orthodox thought of the sixteenth century. We, for example, think of charity as 'self-denial'. We oppose the claims of others to the claims of ourselves as if they were mutu-ally exclusive. Similarly, we tend to regard the group as the natural oppressor of the self, and the self as the natural enemy of the community. The 'theology of Nature' argues in an opposite sense. Love of God, of one's neighbour, and of one's self form a unitary mode of being. 'Selflessness' is an aspect of 'selfishness'. Neighbourliness is coupled in the way of Nature with self-love. Dante makes the point in his *Convivio*:

. . . the proper love of myself, which is the beginning of all the rest; even as everyone perceives that there is no more legitimate nor more gracious method of a man doing honour to himself than by honouring his friend.

It is axiomatic for Dante that 'every man is naturally friendly to every man'. In the same way 'Kinde' was the Middle English for 'Nature', and kindness a natural characteristic of men. In Hooker's view Christ's two commandments are approvable by the Light of Nature and Reason. Of the second commandment he says:

. . . the like natural inducement hath brought men to know that it is their duty no less to love others than themselves. For seeing those things which are equal must needs have all one measure; if I cannot but wish to receive all good, even as much at everyman's hand as any man can wish unto his own soul, how should I look to have any part of my desire herein satisfied, unless myself be careful to satisfy the like desire which is undoubtedly in other men, we all being of one and the same nature?

Gerard Winstanley argued from this to primitive communism, but otherwise both he and Hooker digged the same intellectual common:

> . . . act righteousnesse to all fellow creatures; till the ground accord-ing to Reason; use the labour of your cattell with Reason; follow your course of trading in righteousnesse, as Reason requires, do to men and women as you would have them do to you; and by so doing you shall act as Reasonable creatures, you shall act according to the creation of a man, and so pay the King of Righteousnesse his due.
>
> *Qn.*: Thus the heathen walked according to the light of nature, but Christians must live above nature?
>
> *Ans.*: Then English Christians are in a lower and worser condition than the heathens, for they do not so much. . . . But let me tell you, that man whosoever he be, that is not careful to look into the light of this nature, and follow the rules of that light, to do so he would be done unto, shall never come to see the Spirit, that made and that dwells in nature, which is the Father of the whole creation.

The self that we must act to preserve is that self 'according to the creation of a man'. This is the normative image of man. Com-pared with it all other selves are non-selves, undignified, dis-honourable, and corrupted parodies of human nature.

What critics have called Cordelia's 'pride' in the first scene is therefore merely the Dantesque 'selfishness' framed in Nature and Reason. She is acting 'according to the creation of a man' in a situation where both her father and her sisters act otherwise. She expresses 'the natural virtue' which was incarnated also in the 'Lives' Walton took for his subject matter, and which ani-mated the common men that worked St. George's Heath with Winstanley. Both her sweetness and her strength come from the medieval tradition preserved almost intact by the Elizabethan Establishment.

The apparently proud isolation of Cordelia in the first scene is only one aspect of 'the proper love of myself'. The other aspect of the same central unity which she represents is her compas-sionate move to redeem the state and restore her father. The important point is this: the traditional view sees the self related to a community of human kind. Only in full mutuality can the single nature be fulfilled and finally satisfied. No one can be good to himself alone. Two things follow from this. First, any lesion in the community will involve a dislocation in the individual. Second, proper love of the self is a pre-requisite for proper love of one's neighbour. It is the normative image in man and in the commonweal that must be preserved.

This pervasive mutuality is essential in the Law of Nature. And it is in this sense that Cordelia allegorically is the root of individual sanity as well as social. Lear's rejection of her has thus a twofold significance.

Cordelia's invasion of Britain is simply right. It is of a piece with the rest of her conduct—firm, unconfused, quietly assured:

MESSENGER: News, Madam,
      The British powers are marching hitherward.
CORDELIA: 'Tis Known before. Our preparation stands
      In expectation of them. O dear father,
      It is thy business that I go about: therefore great France
      My mourning and importun'd tears hath pitied:
      No blown ambition doth our armes incite,
      But love, dear love, and our ag'd fathers right:
      Soon may I hear, and see him.   (IV, iv.)

Cordelia's army combines 'Powers from home, and discontents at home'. But the rebellion is amply sanctioned. Cordelia's speech itself has the force of prayer.

Cordelia is Shakespeare's version of singleness and integration. Such studies are difficult to define or discuss directly. We are almost forced to fall back on a *via negativa*, or into the hyperbolical language of some Coleridgean contraries. The impression Cordelia makes is emphatically one of unity. She seems to reconcile opposites: she is passion and order, innocence and maturity, defencelessness and strength, daughter and mother, maid and wife. Shakespeare, fortunately, makes his own definitions. He has his own idiom for handling that unity which the mind more usually conceives as a balance of contraries. Cordelia is described as no one else is in the play:

KENT: Did your letters pierce the Queen to any demonstration
          of grief?

GENTLEMAN: I say she took them, read them in my presence,
      And now and then an ample tear trill'd down
      Her delicate cheek, it seem'd she was a Queen
      Over her passion, who most rebel-like,
      Sought to be King o'er her.

KENT: O then it moved her.

GENTLEMAN: Not to a rage, patience and sorrow strove
      Who should express her goodliest, you have seen
      Sunshine and rain at once, her smiles and tears
      Were like a better way: those happy smilets
      That play'd on her ripe lip seem'd not to know,
      What guests were in her eyes which parted thence,
      As pearls from diamonds dropp'd; in brief,
      Sorrow would be a rarity most beloved,
      If all could so become it.

KENT: Made she no verbal question?

GENTLEMAN: 'Faith once or twice she heav'd the name of father,
      Pantingly forth as if it press'd her heart,
      Cried sisters, sisters, shame of Ladies, sisters:
      Kent, father, sisters, what i' the storm i' th' night;
      Let pity not be believ'd, there she shook
      The holy water from her heavenly eyes,
      And clamour moisten'd her; then away she started,
      To deal with grief alone.   (IV, iii).

The imagery of the passage is the imagery of Nature, of the Nature whose essential expression is an ideal humanity, and of the Nature which—as human—combines also with the nature of weather and seasons, pearls and diamonds. We are soon to see Cordelia as a kind of beneficent Goddess of Nature, whose tears (different from the rain that once wet Lear) can renew and quicken the virtue of earth:

> All blest secrets,
> All you unpublish'd virtues of the earth
> Spring with my tears; be aidant and remediate
> In this good man's distress.   (IV. iv.)

What we see here is Nature as queenly womanhood. April

sunshine and rain at once are merely ancillary to the play of expression in the smiles and tears of a human face. And while the order of the inner-world of feeling is described, the outer order of the political sphere is not forgotten. Cordelia's control of passion is a successful conquest of rebellion:

> . . . it seemed she was a Queen
> Over her passion, who most rebel-like
> Sought to be King o'er her.

It is this capacity for queenly control that makes her different altogether from the king her father. The passionate Lear who had once sought to impose an absolute authority on this queen is brought vividly to mind again: and in the same moment our memory of his madness and his wanderings that followed as a consequence, and our recognition that the daughter he banished is now returning to his aid. External and internal, past and present, are woven together as the unity of Nature requires.

Kent, in his average man's hastiness, assumes that Cordelia was overcome. The Gentleman corrects him—how much or what she felt is not the point. Cordelia felt nothing, or not at all:

> It seemed she was a Queen
> Over her passion.

Yet feeling was wonderfully released: not rage, however:

> . . . patience and sorrow strove
> Who should express her goodliest.

Patience is the clue to that wisdom which outdoes the machiavel's cunning—'the most precious pearl', as Coverdale calls it, the essential Christian insight. Sorrow is both the natural sympathy of a daughter, and also natural compassion 'according to the creation of a man'. In view of the compulsive overflow of pity, it would be just as inappropriate to talk of self-possession in regard to Cordelia's attitude here. Feeling was wonderfully released:

> Faith once or twice she heav'd the name of father
> Pantingly forth as if it press'd her heart,
> Cried sisters, sisters, shame of Ladies' sisters:
> Kent, father, sisters, what i' the storm i' the night.

The passion flows with richness and force, but Cordelia is larger than any of the separable feelings. A conflict of feelings, a balance of feelings, a confusion of feelings, or a blend of feelings —all these are inadequate formulae to describe what is happening. Feelings in her are loyal servants running eagerly to do her will, but always to bring out her beauty and queenliness of state:

> . . . patience and sorrow strove
> Who should express her goodliest.

Or they are clumsy portrait painters making poor copies of the singleness and rich unity which is their model.

The picture of Nature at work is almost finished, except that no image can express her completely. The nearest approach, and the Gentleman's confession of inadequacy, comes in what immediately follows:

> . . . you have seen
> Sunshine and rain at once, her smiles and tears
> Were like a better way.

Cordelia herself, in her integrity, is the 'better way'. Feelings and thoughts, like smiles and tears, are snapped strands of that 'way'. The Gentleman who has undertaken to describe this Cordelia is the same who said of Lear:

> . . . thou hast a daughter
> Who redeems Nature from the general curse
> Which twain have brought her to. (IV, vi.)

Against Cordelia as Shakespeare's picture of integration we might place Shakespeare's version of disintegration—Goneril:

ALBANY: O Goneril,
> You are not worth the dust which the rude wind
> Blows in your face. I fear your disposition:

That nature which contemns i' th' origin
Cannot be border'd certain in itself;
She that herself will sliver and disbranch
From her material sap, perforce must wither,
And come to deadly use.

GONERIL: No more, the text is foolish.

ALBANY: Wisdom and goodness, to the vile seem vile,
Filths savour but themselves . . .
If that the heavens do not their visible spirits
Send quickly down to take this vile offence,
It will come,
Humanity must perforce prey on itself
Like monsters of the deep.

(IV, ii.)

Goneril is one who 'contemns i' th' origin'. She rejects the axiom that 'everyman is naturally friendly to everyman'. She is a branch violently tearing herself away from the tree, Nature, and thence withering and becoming poisonous. Her action will be that of a river overflowing its banks—formless and destructive. Having denied her participation in the limiting, realizing, organizing community of Nature she will lose human identity. Goneril strikes us as a simple efficient social machine. It is interesting that Shakespeare saw her as a bit of chaos, her vitalism of lust and power a withered branch torn from the tree. As such she is vividly contrasted with Cordelia.

A final comment on Cordelia's significance in relation to the rest of the play might be made. We have argued that she is intended for a fully human integration—both a personal integration, and the integration of perfect community. She constitutes the apex of the pyramid. Another step will bring us to the sphere of Bacon's transcendents. That step is taken, I think, in Shakespeare's thought, and in the imagery of his verse. When Lear awakes and sees his daughter he exclaims:

You do me wrong to take me out o' th' grave,
Thou art a soul in bliss, but I am bound
Upon a wheel of fire, that mine own tears
Do scald, like molten lead. (IV, vii.)

The imagery suggests at least this—Cordelia is on a different plane from Lear, not tied to the wheel on which Lear has been bound, nor to that which the Fool thinks is the very mechanism of reality. And this is true in a more general sense. Because Cordelia is full integration she is thereby opposed to every other figure in the play. Each of these others is either an example of disintegration (like Edmund and the Sisters) or of partial integration (like Lear and Edgar). The usual twofold account of the play must therefore be replaced by a threefold one. Cordelia's simplicity stands over against a realm of radical duplicity, and this latter is split in half. On one side is the duplicity of the wicked and machiavellian. On the other is the duplicity of the good—Lear's regeneration that is scarred with remorse and guilt; Edgar's pliability and winding virtue that must bide its time underneath a disguise.

As representing Nature in its communal aspect Cordelia is also contrasted with the societies of Edmund and of Lear. Edmund's is the society of the New Man and the New Age: it is a society based on unfettered competition, and the war of all against all. Lear's is the feudal state in decomposition. It is imperfect in its form and operation (Edmund is a product of its imperfection), but it pays nominal allegiance at least to Nature and Kindness. Of this Nature and Kindness Cordelia is the full realization. She is the norm by which the wrongness of Edmund's world and the imperfection of Lear's is judged. Cordelia fights on her father's behalf, because the medieval world contained at least the seed and recognition of true humanness in society: the advance beyond capitalism will appear in part a return. Cordelia, however, stands for no historically realizable arrangement. Her perfection of truth, justice, charity requires a New Jerusalem. She is in a transcendent relation to the political and the private. She is the norm itself. As such she belongs to the utopian dream of the artist and of the good man.

In a play that is rich in imaginative moments there is one that stands out for its unobtrusiveness and most lucid depth. Captive good is attending Captain ill. Nature is seen standing between the two half-natures: the one a perverse foe, the other a wayward and frail dependant:

Enter in conquest with drum and colours, Bastard, Lear and Cordelia, as prisoners, Soldiers, Captain.

BASTARD: Some officers take them away: good guard,
Until their greater pleasures first be known
That are to censure them.

CORDELIA: We are not the first,
Who with best meaning have incurred the worst:
For thee oppressed King I am cast down,
Myself could else out-frown false Fortune's frown.
Shall we not see these daughters, and these sisters?

LEAR: No, no, no, no: come let's away to prison,
We two alone will sing like birds i' th' cage:
When thou dost ask me blessing, I'll kneel down
And ask of thee forgiveness: so we'll live,
And pray, and sing, and tell old tales, and laugh
At gilded butterflies: and hear (poor rogues)
Talk of Court news, and we'll talk with them too,
Who loses, and who wins; who's in, who's out;
And take upon's the mystery of things,
As if we were God's spies: and we'll wear out
In a wall'd prison, packs and sects of great ones,
That ebb and flow by th' moon.

BASTARD: Take them away.

LEAR: Upon such sacrifices, my Cordelia,
The Gods themselves throw incense. Have I caught thee?
He that parts us, shall bring a brand from Heaven
And fire us hence, like foxes: wipe thine eyes,
The good-years shall devour them, flesh and fell,
Ere they shall make us weep:
We'll see 'em starve first: come.
Exeunt Lear and Cordelia guarded.

(V, iii.)

The scene is marked by another of Lear's great speeches, but it is Cordelia who carries it off—the working of charity that, again, could be mistaken for something hard and automatic had we not a knowledge by this time of the integration such charity implies:

> For thee oppressed King I am cast down,
> Myself could else out-frown false Fortune's frown

—dignity, strength, simplicity, courage, straightness of spine:

> Shall we not see these daughters and these sisters?

—all contrasted on the one hand with Lear's escapism:

> No, no, no, no: come let's away to prison.

and on the other with Edmund's contemptuous indifference:

> Take them away.

It is an image of Nature in action.

CHAPTER IV

KILLING THE KING

The pattern of Shakespeare's chronicle plays develops round the theme of Killing the King. The same theme gives continuity to the plays of the tragic period. *King Lear* gives his theme its fullest and final treatment. (*Macbeth* is prior to *King Lear* in logical order, and may actually precede it in time.) To see the play aright, therefore, we have to put it in the perspective of Shakespeare's tragedies from 1600–1606. It is then seen, in a real sense, as an end. Shakespeare has been moving to this end maybe for the whole of his dramatic career. And when the end is reached it is both a fulfilment and a conclusion. No more Kings are killed in Shakespeare's plays after *King Lear*. It is as if Shakespeare were satisfied that he had at last given the theme adequate statement. The play brings together all that had previously been expressed either fragmentarily or confusedly. The confused and fragmentary receive their lucid order and right positioning. The result is then what we might expect from such a teleology: *King Lear* explains *Julius Caesar* and *Hamlet* and *Macbeth* more readily than they explain it.

I propose to give a rapid sketch of the series. It is only the skeleton of each play that such a sketch will be able to indicate. However, the skeleton will be a real structure, not an arbitrary selection of odd bones. It will show the significant framework of the tragic period. In addition, there should be no chance of confusing such a bare summary with any judicial treatment of each play. (Although Shakespeare, I think, is feeling his way constantly towards an end, he is a cat that always falls on its feet. At each stage he is able to achieve an apparently final and highly skilful balance. So that each play can be regarded, if we like, as an end in itself: a complete individual study.) Finally, it will be clearer from such a summary how *King Lear* brings the bones together, and which bones are used, to be given the new life.

[a]

JULIUS CAESAR

In *Julius Caesar* Caesar himself is the good King. He is good on the evidence of those qualities and achievements which cause the crown to be offered to him in the first place. The will made known after his death clinches the fact of his royal magnanimity. The King-slayer is Brutus: a good-hearted man, and the hero of the play, but compromised by his association with the conspirators. The hero is a tool in their hands. Like Hamlet and Othello after him, Brutus's difficulty is that he cannot tell the truth from the perfect imitation. Cassius and the conspirators use the machiavellian device. They find it easy to suggest that the good ruler is himself really a villain, an exquisite hypocrite able by flawless acting to cover up sinister designs. The tables are turned on the conspirators by the one man in the play who can beat them at their own machiavellian game. Antony is a machiavel *par excellence*, but in the Falconbridge tradition. He moves to rescue the state from chaos. Whereas Cassius and the conspirators, through intimate knowledge of his make-up, can make one man their tool, Antony can just as easily wind the whole Roman mob round his little finger. He is not, however, sinister. Both his love of Caesar and his loyalty are warm and genuine. And his motive in thwarting the conspiracy is above suspicion. It is the public order which must be safeguarded at all costs.

On the question of killing the King the play gives a single

counsel. If the King is really bad the good man will feel it his duty to murder him. In this, moreover, he will be justified. Shakespeare has detached himself from the Homilies' doctrine of passive obedience. (To do so with impunity he had to leave English history for Roman.) The difficulty is, however, that the good man can easily be a dupe. Such goodness as Brutus's is a liability rather than an asset so long as it cannot tell the appearance from the reality. It becomes one element more in the confusion that is always threatening good order. All unconscious, it can be used as a stalking horse by the evil-doer. Better, therefore, trust to the expert knower of man, the one who knows that man is at heart an anti-social creature, the one who will neither be blinded by stupid self-seeking nor confused by impossible idealism. The politically operative parts of man being greed for power and curious cunning, it is safer to be in the hands of the machiavel who is efficient and benevolently disposed, who will at least keep good order, and—his own coinciding here with the public interest—secure quiet maybe even with justice.

The plot of the play brings about the deaths of the King and his murderer. Both casualties are incidental to the basic struggle. This is the contest between the rival machiavellisms, the sinister and the benign. At the end of the play the good King and the good man and the defeated conspirators are all dead. Mark Antony is left in cool and unshakable control, decisive commander of the political realm, a Henry V with no pretensions to holiness but with no Falstaff on his conscience.

It might be said that in this *Julius Caesar* reaches a nugatory conclusion. It achieves political comedy at the expense of private tragedy. The truth is that the figures of the grand theme are not shown in their most fertile relationships. The theme, as a result, never reaches its proper grandeur.

The most interesting roles of the machiavel hitherto have been, first, that of diabolical villain in the political sphere, and, second, that of heroic saviour of the state. As villain and devil we knew that the machiavel was pitted against a King who stood for 'the life, the right, and truth of all this realm.' Meaning of a metaphysical order accrued to his actions immediately. The nature affronted by the machiavel's action as well as the nature expressed in it must both be weighed. As heroic saviour, on the other hand, the machiavel is again drawn into a circle where politics cannot be discussed without considering also the order to which goodness belongs. The line of machiavels from Falconbridge represents Shakespeare's effort unsuccessfully to argue for the superiority of the political virtues in their own right. Political effectiveness denotes moral superiority. The King must be strong before he can be good.

Antony is a machiavel of neither the one type nor the other. While he remains the benevolent machiavel and rescues the state from chaos, Antony suffers the withdrawal of Shakespeare's enthusiasm and approbation. Antony is not made the hero of the play. Shakespeare seems content now to make a diminished claim for the type. There is no pretence in *Julius Caesar* that the political virtues can compete with the goodness Brutus stands for, much less replace it. And at the same time Shakespeare refrains from presenting Antony in any diabolical light. It is simply that Antony's world and that of Brutus are entirely separate. Antony will never try to reconcile them: that is what makes him wise and successful. Brutus, in trying to relate the two, almost ruins the state and certainly destroys himself.

The situation we are left in is thus an intellectual and moral cul-de-sac. Antony's 'order' is at best a negative thing. It is only good by comparison with some Hobbesian 'state of war' it might prevent. Antony is not a conscious theorist. He acts, however, on a view of man's nature and man's role in society which, if he were, would bring him into conflict with the goodness Brutus represents. That goodness itself, on the other hand, is a barren and futile thing. Brutus is as politically ineffective as Henry VI and as functionally irrelevant. The situation for goodness has, in fact, deteriorated since the early chronicle plays. It can muster no party in the state now. And because of its fatal inability to detect the fake from the genuine, it can be used as a tool and factor of wickedness. Its presence in the state only makes knavery doubly dangerous.

The separation of the moral and political spheres leads therefore to an impossible dichotomy. The balance of the play is a delusive and a faked stability. The problems implicit are only made more urgent by this false resolution.

On the positive side, however, it is possible to see Shakespeare moving forward in *Julius Caesar* to his final solutions. After his unsuccessful attempts to unite them in a single person, he has again separated out the figures of the good man and the machiavel. To that extent *Julius Caesar* harks back to the universe of *Henry VI* and looks forward to that of *King Lear*. Secondly, the goodness is by intention positive and political: it moves to convert 'good order' into something better. It is right to do this even if a King must be killed. Furthermore, though in this he is deceived, the good man thinks he is murdering a machiavel-King. The throne and machiavellism are an intolerable conjunction. The machiavel's claim to command the political sphere cannot therefore go unquestioned. This is Richard III and Richmond as well as Edmund and Edgar. However, Brutus is really deceived. He is not, as he thinks, an agent, he is a tool. His holy crusade is really a mean conspiracy. It is not Caesar who is the machiavel but Cassius. Goodness is not politically trustworthy while it can be so profoundly gulled. It can safeguard other's welfare no more than it can ensure its own.

This problem of the difference, for practical purposes, between the truth and the perfect imitation now becomes almost all-absorbing for Shakespeare. It is the problem with which *King Lear* begins in the first act. Lear himself comes to a solution which, in his case, is a 'feeling' knowledge: the infallible fruit of bitter experience, long suffering, and patience. Gloster corrects the same fault of vision by a similar education. It may be therefore that Shakespeare ultimately came to regard the problem as soluble. It is not solved, however, in *Julius Caesar*. For that reason the machiavellism which rigs the game plays the game out by itself. And where there is only one real contestant that one must win. Machiavellism therefore does win, and Antony is left master of the field. But it is a hollow victory.

A final symbol of goodness's self-frustration is Brutus's self-slaughter. A final testimony to the futility of the machiavel's victory is the epitaph Antony utters:

> This was the Noblest Roman of them all;
> All the Conspirators save only hee,
> Did that they did, in envy of great *Caesar*:
> He, onely in a generall honest thought,
> And common good to all, made one of them.
> His life was gentle, and the Elements
> So mixt in him, that Nature might stand up,
> And say to all the world; This was a man.
>
> (*Julius Caesar*, V, v.)

[b]

HAMLET

Hamlet is characterized chiefly by excess. The excess is an *embarras de richesses*, and criticism recently has tended to stress the embarrassment rather than the riches. The play has too much story and too many people; yet there is not enough story to explain all the people, and not enough people to tell the whole story. The effects gained are those of a brilliant opportunism. Shakespeare lends his pen to every occasion regardless. One result is that *Hamlet* contains more quotable phrases than any other of Shakespeare's plays, and more memorable scenes. Another result is a sense of bewilderment. In spite of all the things that are crowded in and which we would not be without, there is so much that seems to have been crowded out which we could certainly do with. The play has everything that Shakespeare can give, except the final synthesis: no one has been satisfied with Horatio's summary:

> . . . give order that these bodies
> High on a stage be placed to the view;
> And let me speake to th' yet unknowing world,
> How these things came about. So shall you heare
> Of carnall, bloudie, and unnaturall acts;
> Of accidentall judgements, casuall slaughters;
> Of deaths put on by cunning, and forc'd cause,
> And, in this upshot, purposes mistooke
> Falne on the Inventors' heads: All this can I
> Truly deliver. (*Hamlet*, V, ii.)

Hamlet mingles the familiar and the unfamiliar. The familiar matter is the old story of killing the King. The new matter results from the introduction of Gertrude (the hero's mother) and Ophelia (his forsaken sweetheart) into the old framework.

As in *Julius Caesar* and *Macbeth* the stage is set by the murder of a good King. The act, bloody in itself, is rendered unnatural by the king-slayer's being brother to the murdered King. It becomes carnal when the murderer marries his victim's wife. The rightful King has thus been slain and the throne is occupied by a machiavel. Originally such an unnatural act and such a usurpation of authority would entail a profound disturbance to the state. In this instance, however, we are not made aware of any ill-effects. The first scene echoes with the noise of ship-building and armament manufacturing—the background against which the ghost walks—and Horatio is old-fashioned enough to be of the opinion:

> This boades some strange erruption to our State.
> (*Hamlet*, I, i.)

But the second scene shows Claudius competently handling the threat of war. In despatching the ambassadors to Norway he is both firm and diplomatic. Fortinbras is mistaken if he imagines

Our State to be disjoynt, and out of Frame.
(*Hamlet*, I, ii.)

Whatever might be rotten in the state of Denmark there are no obvious repercussions in the sphere of public life or of the general weal. What has happened, of course, is that Shakespeare is treating the killing of a King as a merely private murder. To everyone except Hamlet Claudius is as good as his predecessor. Hamlet's mother certainly thinks so.

This is a new feature in Shakespeare's handling of the theme, and it is only one of several. It may be the need he felt to give the revived play an infusion of novelty, but each time a familiar role appears an unfamiliar type is made to fill it. This is one of the causes of confusion in *Hamlet*: the stock story, which seems to demand the stock characters and the stock motives, is supplied with neither. The play lacks Shakespeare's usual degree of co-operation between story and characterization and underlying thought.

This is most obvious in the figure of the wrongful King. We called Claudius a machiavel for the sake of convenience, and that is certainly how he is first thought of by Hamlet:

> Oh Villaine, Villaine, smiling damned Villaine!
> My Tables, my Tables; meet it is I set it downe,
> That one may smile and smile and be a Villaine.
> (*Hamlet*, I, v.)

He has the machiavel's cunning (the 'witchcraft of his wits'), the same ability to simulate the appearance of virtue, and like Richard III he can persuade his victim's wife to marry him. Like Richard, too, he uses a pair of tool-villains. But the machiavel-King proper, in Shakespeare, is a public and political menace as well as a confessed and obdurate villain. Claudius is neither. He is uxorius, for one thing. He is also anxious to become good. His crime weighs heavily upon him and it is obvious that he is more tender-hefted than a King-slayer should be. When

148

Polonius moralizes on hypocrisy, Claudius reveals his billious-
ness of conscience:

POLONIUS: Ophelia . . . Reade on this booke,
           That shew of such an exercise may colour
           Your lonelinesse. We are oft to blame in this,
           'Tis too much prov'd, that with Devotions visage,
           And pious Action, we do sugre o're
           The divell himselfe.
KING: Oh 'tis true:
           How smart a lash that speech doth give my Conscience!
           The Harlot's Cheeke beautied with plaist'ring Art
           Is not more ugly to the thing that helpes it,
           Then is my deede, to my most painted word.
           O heavie burthen!   (*Hamlet*, III, i.)

Claudius's crime sickens him. His attempt to re-establish himself through prayer is sincere if unsuccessful. He knows the price
of atonement, but his sick will is incapable of paying it; he cannot shake off pride, he cannot relinquish the throne, and especially he cannot part with Gertrude. Claudius's apparent piety is
not, therefore, the same as Richard's bible-reading. Even his
good advice to Hamlet in Act I, scene iii, and his general solici-
tude for Hamlet's well-being, is mixed with honest concern. It
is motivated by love for Hamlet's mother as much as by anxiety
for his own safety. If it is hypocrisy it is that sort which most
sincerely flatters virtue. If he is a machiavel, Claudius is a machiavel in carpet slippers—an essential contradiction.

Yet Claudius has to go through with the role of machiavel-
King and with the villainy of plotting against the life of the
rightful heir. Again, however, there is a central dislocation.
Claudius never has the initiative in his plot against the Prince's
life as he evidently must have had in that against the King's.
Hamlet forces him each step towards the second crime. As
Claudius is presented in Shakespeare's play he is a man who cannot get rid of his past acting under the compulsion of old habits
he would gladly slough. If we peer into the seeds of his story

we can see curious analogies. Claudius as the machiavel whose conscience awakes is Richard on the eve of Bosworth. Claudius slaying Hamlet's father originally, Claudius weighed upon by inordinate love of Gertrude, Claudius pressed along the road of subsequent wickedness by a force outside himself which is at the same time a consequence of his past action, is Macbeth. Claudius, finally, as the sick King on the throne is Lear, though a Lear frustrated. For Lear achieves regeneration: he is the bad King and the good King together, bound up in a single nature. And the king Lear removes from the throne (thereby laying open the kingdom to the disastrous rule of the avowed and diabolical machiavels) is himself. But before Shakespeare can make such a readjustment and synthesis he will have to investigate more fully the component natures of man.

The transfer of the killing of the King from the public sphere to the purely private thus leads to an extensive reshaping of the King-machiavel. Claudius has to perform all the stock actions required by the story without having the stock character appropriate to them. A similar modification, and a similar disparity of story and character, is perceptible in the figure of the good man who is opposed to the wicked usurper.

While the slaying of the bad King was a public duty there was an unambiguous motive for heroic action. Brutus responds to the demands of public-spiritedness, and is driven to heroic disaster by it. Prince Hamlet cannot have Brutus's motive. For Claudius the murdered man is more significant as a brother than as a King, and for Hamlet it is a father he has lost rather than a good sovereign the state has been deprived of. The play to that extent is a private tragedy enacted in court dress on a public stage.

At the same time, however, Hamlet, too, must go through the motions of the story. His role requires him to be the man entrusted with the task of killing the King, to restore righteousness to the order of things as well as to revenge his father. It is a machiavel-King, and a King-slayer, Hamlet sees himself opposed to. His problem is to devise a strategy that will circumvent the machiavel's.

This strategy is, of course, that of feigned madness. The good man will outdo the machiavel. He will steal the machiavel's main weapon and be an even more proficient self-disguiser. Hamlet's 'antic disposition' is such a disguise, or series of disguises. From this point of view the play could well have resolved itself into a contest between the feigned madman and the supreme hyprocrite: a tug-of-war which could have been maintained with wavering fortunes and without any unnecessary delays for the whole of the five acts. The play, of course, as we know, is not only this, but it is partly this. And the part is important. Brutus's shortcoming was his lack of the machiavel's insight; this made him a pipe for the conspirators to play on. Hamlet will not have this weakness, as Rosencrantz and Guildenstern discover:

> There's letters seal'd: and my two schoolfellows—
> Whom I will trust as I will adders fang'd—
> They bear the mandate; they must sweep my way
> And marshal me to Knavery. Let it work;
> For 'tis the sport to have the engineer
> Hoist with his own petard: and't shall go hard
> But I will delve one yard below their mines,
> And blow them at the moon: O, 'tis most sweet,
> When in one line two crafts directly meet.
>
> (*Hamlet*, III, v.)

Hamlet is the machiavel of goodness at a new level. Just as Henry V conflated Henry VI and Richard, Shakespeare seems determined not to leave affairs in the impasse of *Julius Caesar*. The good man must be equipped with the armoury of machiavellism. This, too, is carried over into *King Lear* and there given a final form. The analogy to Hamlet (this part of him) is Edgar. Edgar's serial changes of shape are rapid symbolizations and also swiftly adopted antic dispositions. We might note, however, *King Lear's* seeming judgment on *Hamlet*. It would appear that the *Hamlet* solution was a mistaken one. The good man, as Edgar, does not directly meet the machiavel in the same line of craft. Instead of head-on collision, we have evasion. The good man would be deluded, anyway, to commit everything to a contest of cunning. It is risky to play the machiavel at his own game, with his own weapons, and according to his own rules. It is, moreover, something contaminating to undertake. Both Cordelia and Edgar disdain to enter the competition. Edgar's disguises are therefore protective colouring. Instead of trusting to his wits, he trusts to patience and that process of providence or time which he calls 'ripeness'. When the time is ripe, he will reveal himself. He will have remained meanwhile uncontaminated. Most important of all he will choose the occasion; it will not be chosen for him by an opponent he cannot trust: 'ripeness is all'. By this unambiguous and successful strategy he will overcome the machiavel. At the end of the play he will be made King. This wisdom is a deeper craft than cunning.

The other feature of the machiavel matter—the ability to confound the perfect imitation and the truth—pervades almost the whole of *Hamlet*. It is given comic statement in Polonius who imputes hypocrisy to Hamlet's sincere love:

> Doe not beleeve his vowes; for they are Broakers,
> Not of the eye, which their Investments show:
> But meere implorators of unholy Sutes,
> Breathing like sanctified and pious bonds,
> The better to beguile.   (*Hamlet*, I, iii.)

Polonius prides himself on his machiavellian insight into human nature and on his machiavellian skill in juggling with the lie and the truth:

> See you now;
> Your bait of falshood, takes this Cape of truth;
> And thus doe we of wisedome and of reach
> With windlesses, and with assaies of Bias,
> By indirections finde directions out.   (*Hamlet*, II, i.)

Polonius has the theory to perfection. But the joke is that his practice of it is pathetic., He mistakes Hamlet entirely, and is killed for his mistake while hiding behind the arras.

The same confusion of appearance and reality is reflected ironically in Hamlet himself. Hamlet is going to vie with the machiavel in dissembling, but almost his first line in the play is:

> Seemes Madam? Nay, it is: I know not seemes.
> *(Hamlet, I, ii.)*

It crops up as a problem in connection with the Ghost and is the reason Hamlet needs supplementary proof that what the Ghost alleges is true:

> The Spirit that I have seene
> May be the Divell, and the Divel hath power
> T'assume a pleasing shape, yea and perhaps
> Out of my Weaknesse, and my Mellancholly,
> As he is very potent with such Spirits,
> Abuses me to damne me. Ile have grounds
> More Relative then this: the Play's the thing,
> Wherein Ile catch the Conscience of the King.
> *(Hamlet, II, ii.)*

That we cannot know truth from a lie even where our know-ledge surely must be most intimate is the main shock in what the Ghost reveals:

> GHOST: But know thou Noble youth,
> The Serpent that did sting thy Fathers life,
> Now wears his Crowne.
> HAMLET: O my Propheticke soule: mine Uncle?
> GHOST: I that incestuous, that adulterate Beast
> With witchcraft of his wits, hath Traitorous guifts.
> Oh wickedWit, and Gifts, that have the power
> So to seduce? won to this shameful Lust
> The will of my most seeming vertuous Queene:
> Oh *Hamlet*, what a falling off was there,
> From me, whose love was of that dignity,
> That it went hand in hand, even with the Vow
> I made to her in Marriage; and to decline
> Upon a wretch, whose Naturall gifts were poore
> To those of mine. But Vertue, as it never will be moved,

Though Lewdnesse court it in a shape of Heaven:
So Lust, though to a radiant Angell link'd
Will sate itself in a Celestiall bed, and prey on Garbage.
(*Hamlet*, I, iv.)

The problem of the lie and the truth was originally tied to the problem of machiavellism. Now it is detached from this special problem and made general. It is not only that the declared villain can wear the mask of virtue. People we have known all our lives may not be what they seem. All appearances may be deceptive, and best safety, as Laertes advises Ophelia, lie in fear. The very bases of human confidence can be shaken by this doubt, and decisive action in this treacherous world of shadows become impossible. If Shakespeare had amplified this theme there would again have been matter enough to explain Hamlet's delay. The Hamlet problem would then have been, how to justify any action at all, except suicide. As it is, the radical doubt does affect the portrayal of the Prince. His reaction after mistaking the lie in Gertrude for the truth is to take Ophelia's truth for a lie. This is the explanation of 'Get thee to a Nunnery':

If thou doest marry, Ile give thee this Plague for thy Dowrie. Be thou as chast as Ice, as pure as Snow, thou shalt not escape Calumny. Get thee to a Nunnery. Go, Farewell. Or if thou wilt needs Marry, marry a fool: for Wise Men know well enough, what monsters you make of them. To a Nunnery go, and quickly too. Farewell.... Go too, Ile no more on't, it hath made me mad. I say, we will have no more Marriages. Those that are married already, all but one shall live, the rest shall keep as they are. To a Nunnery, go. (*Hamlet*, III, i.)

Lear, in his madness, contemplates womankind in the same way; though his advice is vindictively the opposite of Hamlet's —'To't luxury, pell-mell'.

It is, of course, because we find a dubious double nature in ourselves first that we are all the more apt to give weight to the imputation of duplicity in others, and to question the public face presented to the world by our neighbours:

Get thee to a Nunnerie. Why would'st thou be a breeder of Sinners?

I am my selfe indifferent honest, but yet I could accuse me of such things, that it were better my mother had not borne me. I am very prowd, revengefull, Ambitious, with more offences at my becke, then I have thoughts to put them in, imagination to give them shape, or time to acte them in. What should such Fellowes as I do, crawling betweene Heaven and Earth. We are arrant Knaves all, beleeve none of us. Goe thy ways to a Nunnery. (*Hamlet*, III, i.)

The singleness of being Hamlet wants, or the doubleness he wants to be rid of, is something that cannot be found in the action proposed to him as a moral duty—if it can be found in any action at all. This is another of Shakespeare's casually dropped profundities that the play does not fully expand. Though Hamlet may not have the ultimate range or coherence of *King Lear* it has its own metaphysical sweep. Here what is troubling Hamlet is the sense of sin that St. Paul expresses in 'All have offended and have need of the glory of God', a radical imperfection felt even by the saint, which no human action can overcome. The demand to revenge his dead father is only one among innumerable other demands on his nature, and not even the one most relevant to his needs. Hamlet's problem is not the problem of his wasting time. It is the opposite: he has not enough time at his disposal in which to do all that is needful. His delay, therefore, has this possible reason, too. But again it is one which the play does not amplify: for sidelights on the kind of action which is non-action, and the kind of inaction which is action we have to wait until the 'ripeness' of *King Lear*.

This conversion of the machiavellian problem proper into a special case of the more general problem of sin, and the transfer of the King-killing story from the plane of politics to that of private morality, brings us to the final aspect of the play which we wish to include in this summary—the new matter which centres round the play's two women: Hamlet's mother and his mistress. The reason for the appearance of women in Shakespeare's tragedies at this point (there are no dominating women in the essential plot of *Julius Caesar*) is fairly evident. Shakespeare has turned from the political aspect of his theme because he has found the real centre of his problem in the private world of the individual's conscience and the individual's fallibility. He needs Hamlet's love of his mother to replace as a motive the love of justice which operated in Brutus. At the same time the general problem of sin and duplicity can be brought to a sharp focus through the same woman symbols. They look like angels and act like centaurs; or like the Bestiary harpies:

> Ex umbilico sunt ut pulcherrima virgo
> Quod que facit monstrum volucres sunt inde deorsum.

Apart from this function at this point in the tragedy-cycle, both Gertrude and Ophelia are less significant in themselves than they are as auguries of the villainesses and heroines to come. The line from Gertrude goes through Cressida and Lady Macbeth, to Goneril and Regan; that from Ophelia through Desdemona to Cordelia.

Gertrude is one of Shakespeare's more careless productions. She is neither coherently nor clearly presented. The Ghost of Hamlet's father sees her as Lust leaving her celestial bed and, already sated, preying upon garbage: *volucres sunt inde deorsum*. Claudius sees her as a woman he has maybe committed murder for, and whose authority over him is such he will treat her son as tenderly as he can. Hamlet, as we might expect, has both the Ghost's disgust and Claudius's tender affection. In the play Gertrude is seen as a loving mother and a dutiful wife. The difficulty is that she can be as dutiful to the murderer of the King as to the King murdered. Hamlet in the bedroom scene brings her to realize the enormity of her misdeeds, but the play subsequently indicates no change at all in her conduct. To be a clear instance of deceitful appearance Gertrude should of course conform to the Ghost's picture. As it is, a vague positive charge counteracts the negative of her viciousness.

The significant relationship, which Shakespeare's later tragedies develop, is the association of sinister woman with wrongful

King—the final conjunction of Goneril and Regan with Edmund, of Lady Macbeth with Macbeth. The significant development for Ophelia occurs when Shakespeare examines first what happens when a woman 'as chast as Ice, as pure as Snow', actually does marry, and then encounters the inevitable 'Calumny'; next when he submits the same symbol of truth and purity to a similar calumny, illustrates the disastrous consequences for those who do her this wrong, and vindicates such truth and purity as both real and recognizable as such, really appreciated in the end after the experience of living apart from them has been tried. Ophelia's destiny is to become Cordelia after being Desdemona.

A clear line, then, visibly runs through the remaining great plays of the tragic period, and they can be dealt with very briefly. *Hamlet* is characterized by kaleidoscopic richness, a bewildering excess, a brilliant opportunism. Shakespeare seems to spill over in every direction. In the plays that follow the field of vision is contracted, but there is a clearer focus. Shakespeare does not handle so much at once, but what he handles is given ampler and more satisfying treatment. He avoids overcrowding; the plays gain in lucidity, in sense of control, and in form.

[c]

TROILUS AND CRESSIDA

Troilus and Cressida has no machiavel. It takes up the question propounded in *Hamlet* through the action of Gertrude and its effects on her son. Alternatively, we might say, it takes Hamlet's father and Hamlet's mother, makes them of an age with Hamlet and Ophelia, and re-enacts the drama of seeming virtue's horrible falling off. No machiavel is required as villain in such a drama. Human nature to itself rebels with none else near.

Shakespeare returns to the clear pattern of *Julius Caesar*. There are two orders of experience contrasted in the play, analogous to the balance of Brutus against Antony. These are embodied in the Trojan world and the Greek world, and in the supreme examples of each, Troilus and Ulysses. The Trojans are chivalrous idealists, the Greeks practical realists. 'Idealism' and 'realism' may be stupid words for making the appropriate distinction. Some contrast approximating to our 'idealism' and 'realism' is, however, involved. Better terms might be the two 'reasons' we have already examined in connection with the Lear party and the Edmund party; or, maybe better still, Shakespeare's own earlier symbolization of Antony and Brutus. It is two different 'orders' that are at the bottom of the distinction between Trojan and Greek, two different forms of human nature and its world. The Trojan Reason resembles Faith. It is a unity of Reason and Resolve. Its basic instinct is to claim, with Keats, that what the heart feels as Beauty must be truth. It is mingled with the impassioned outgoing side of man—outgoing need that clamours for response. Whatever metaphysical unity there might be in the universe, room will have to be found in that unity for what the heart feels to be most precious and the mind knows immediately to be, in some sense, real. It is an idealism that can organize itself into a community—the community of Troy revolving round Trojan Helen.

This inner order is given precedence in the play over the order, the reason, the unimpassioned matter-of-factness, of Ulysses: Ulysses who subordinates the man to the state, and conceives the state as a Leviathan. The world of Ulysses is a second-best. It is only good for that human nature which has rebelled against itself—those beast-natures which Thersites comments upon:

There's Ulysses and old Nestor, whose wit was mouldy ere their grandsires had nails on their toes, yoke you like draft-Oxen and make you plough up the warre.

Upon defection and self-revolt the Trojan unity can collapse back into Ulysses' order (organizing the beasts into some sort of constraining polity); or, going further still in its recoil, become the scurrilous anarch and contemner Thersites.

The most significant scene in the play, therefore, is not that devoted to Ulysses' speech on Degree, but that in which Troilus sees the falling-off of Cressida. As Troilus watches Cressida with Diomed, Thersites and Ulysses stand on either side of him. Troilus has somehow to meet the shock, and avoid both the alternatives personified on the stage alongside him:

> This she? No this is *Diomeds Cressida*:
> If beau*tie* have a Soule, this is not she:
> If soules guide vowes; if vowes are sanctimonie;
> If sanctimonie be the gods delight:
> If there be rule in unitie it selfe,
> This is not she: O madnesse of discourse!
> That cause sets up, with, and against thy selfe;
> By foule authority: where reason can revolt
> Without perdition, and loss assume all reason,
> Without revolt. This is, and is not *Cressid*:
> Within my soule, there doth conduce a fight
> Of this strange nature, that a thing inseperate
> Divides more wider than the skie and earth:
> And yet the spacious bredth of this division
> Admits no Orifex for a point as subtle,
> As *Ariachnes* broken woofe to enter:
> Instance, O instance! strong as Plutoes gates:
> Cressid is mine, tied with the bonds of heaven;
> Instance, O instance! strong as heaven itself:
> The bonds of heaven are slipt, dissolv'd, and loos'd,
> And with another knot five finger tied,
> The fractions of her faith, orts of her love:
> The fragments, scraps, the bits, the greazy reliques,
> Of her ore-eaten faith, are bound to *Diomed*.
>
> (*Troilus and Cressida*, V, ii.)

Troilus is not, however, like Hamlet, paralysed by the lie. He is an active goodness, and the discovery serves as a spur rather than a clog to his will. He has an adequate outlet and a proper object for his new passion of indignation:

ULYSSES: May worthy *Troilus* be but halfe attached
   With that which here his passion doth expresse?
TROILUS: I, Greeke; and that shall be divulged well
   In Characters, as red as *Mars* his heart
   Inflam'd with *Venus*: never did yong man fancy
   With so eternall and so fixt a soule.
   Harke Greek: as much as I doe *Cressida* love;
   So much by weight, hate I her *Diomed*:
   That Sleeve is mine that heele beare in his Helme;
   Were it a Caske compos'd by *Vulcans* skill,
   My Sword should bite it: Not the dreadful spout,
   Which Shipmen do the Hurricano call,
   Constring'd in masse by the almighty Fenne,
   Shall dizzie with more clamour Neptunes eare
   In his discent, then shall my prompted sword
   Falling on *Diomed*.
THERSITES: Heele tickle it for his concupie.
          (*Troilus and Cressida*, V, ii.)

Troilus's victory is an outcome of that active control, that steadying hold on a wilfully optimistic view of the ultimate outcome of the conflict between truth and the lie, which he calls (like Lear and Gloster after him) 'patience':

   There is betweene my will, and all offences,
   A guard of patience. . . .
     . . . Feare me not, sweete Lord:
   I will not be my selfe, nor have cognition
   Of what I feele: I am all patience.
          (*Troilus and Cressida*, V, ii.)

Such 'patience', of course, Thersites would call 'blind faith'.

[d]

OTHELLO and MACBETH

Othello and *Macbeth* can be dealt with even more summarily. They seem to fall of themselves into the mutually-explanatory series it has been our intention to construct. We have indicated already the matter they extract from the nebular mass of *Hamlet*. *Othello* re-animates the image of the pure woman, *Macbeth* that of the de-natured villainess. *Othello* is marked by the return of the machiavel—a domestic machiavel, because the play (like all the plays since *Julius Caesar*) confines itself to the private aspect of the grand theme. (Private or public in this theme, of course, is a matter of emphasis. *Troilus and Cressida* is essentially private in its emphasis, but only because the metaphysical unity is one which touches the individual first, and is mediated thereafter into the public spheres of Trojan or Greek through the individual experience.) *Macbeth*, however, restores the public aspect to its full scope and importance. Again, it is a King who is killed; and the death and usurpation that follow disrupt the frame of the whole common weal.

Dr. Tillyard has rightly pointed out how nearly the formal outline of *Macbeth* approximates to that of Shakespeare's very earliest chronicle plays. The holy King who represents the stable decencies of the traditional sovereignty; his murderer who is forced to rule with blood and iron, proceeding from enormity to enormity; the eventual mustering of the powers of outraged pity and justice; their return and the overthrow of the ungodly rule—this is also the shape of the first chronicle tetralogy.

But though the form is the same, there is an important difference in content. *Macbeth* reflects the plays of the tragic period that have also preceded it. Thus our interest is centred first on Macbeth's state of mind, and the initial rebellion of his nature which leads to the King-slaying. Shakespeare is concerned not only with the evil man's impact on the world, but also with the manner and process of his entry into evil. So we see Macbeth at first almost equally poised (as anyone might be) between the good and the bad. His wife is highly doubtful of his wickedness:

> . . . yet doe I feare thy Nature,
> It is too full o' th' Milke of humane kindnesse,
> To catch the neerest way. Thou would'st be great;

Art not without Ambition, but without
The illnesse should attend it. What thou would'st highly,
Thou would'st thou holily: would'st not play false,
And yet would'st wrongly winne.

(*Macbeth*, I, v.)

We then see how, his reason having been hypnotized by the fortune-telling witches, he lends his will to the foretold event, and catches the nearest way. The corruption of the individual will is then mediated through action into the political realm. One notable thing is that in the degeneration of a man we watch the procreation of a machiavel—an explanation of the machiavel so to speak, in terms of misuse of the intellect, misdirection of the will, and denial of natural compassion. The machiavel is no longer a monster. He is the final result of a process that can start at any time and in anyone. No special qualifications of bloody-naturedness are required. Animal courage, desperate cruelty, the reckless and frightful power of fear, will all accrue to the individual as the de-humanizing process gathers momentum.

The fact is that the contours of Shakespeare's moral world now seem to have become both steady and firm. In spite of its shadowed margin *Macbeth* gives an impression of settledness and inclusiveness, solidity and depth. The machiavel is not a confusing bogey, and neither is he wished away; he is profoundly understood in his genesis. Similarly the acute anxiety over truth and the appearance of truth seems to have subsided. Deception is still possible, and a real factor in evil is the misuse of wit, and the misdirection of will to wound the vulnerable good, which is characteristic of the machiavel. However, the fact that a lie can trick itself out as a perfect imitation of truth is no longer a reason for flight from truth:

Angels are bright still, though the brightest fell:
Though all things foule would weare the brows of grace,
Yet Grace must still looke so.   (*Macbeth*, IV, iii.)

Truth does not need to forsake its own ground in competition with the windings of policy. It will hold fast in patience until the imitation proves itself, by its fruits, to be what it is. The lines quoted explain Cordelia's conduct in the first scene of *King Lear* more adequately than most of the psychological assessments.

For with *Macbeth* we are on the threshold of the *King Lear* universe.

Maybe the most important discovery in *Macbeth*, which is handed on to *King Lear*, is the usefulness, for displaying Shakespeare's grand theme, of the traditional Christian theology—that theology which, for convenience, we have called the theology of 'Nature'. It is in *Macbeth*, I think, that the discovery is made. Shakespeare now has to hand an intellectual framework which will carry, express, and even elucidate the full story of 'Killing the King'; the theme of Good and Evil in the private and public worlds, under the aspects both of history and eternity; the theme which holds together two double strands—the kingly nature as an individual possibility and as a requirement for decency and justice in the common weal; and, with this, the machiavel nature, a private defection and thereupon a public menace: the theme of religion and politics, of the good man and the bad society. But before tracing the King's course through the territory of the Natures, we might sum up those respects so far indicated in which *King Lear* models a final unity out of the experience of the whole tragic period.

The tragic period begins with two plays given over to radical doubt. One is devoted to the public side of the theme, the other turns away into the private sphere. Both come to an impasse. In *Julius Caesar* goodness is politically ineffectual, the state is altogether dominated by the machiavel. The only hope is that the machiavel will be cunning enough to be also well-disposed. In *Hamlet* paralysis comes from the realization that the mind cannot tell the truth from the seeming-true: action is therefore impossible.

In *Troilus and Cressida* Shakespeare has emerged from the cul-de-sac. The two orders of experience are restored. Balanced against the world of Ulysses and his beef-witted instruments is an order of communal existence different from it and superior to it—the world of Troy. In the private sphere deception is still an admitted possibility, but the hero can survive deception. An outlet for action is left open, even if it is only Troilus destroying Diomed. *Troilus and Cressida* in this represents a return on Shakespeare's part to a qualified moral optimism. The private issue of Troilus' deception dominates the play. The private sphere is primary. What happens on the political plane derives its meaning from what has happened first on the personal. More important still, the integrity of the hero is self sufficient: he can withstand the shock of betrayal.

The private and personal continue to dominate in *Othello*. The image of the pure woman is restored, and the conception of the Kingly nature who is married to her. The integrity of the two is unquestionable and compelling, but not self-sufficient. Their marriage is brought to disaster by Iago. The good could and would stand by itself. It requires, however, a community of goodness in which to be permanent. It is vulnerable so long as there is anywhere around it the intention to wound. Following Troilus in this, neither Othello nor Desdemona have any trace of the machiavellian. Neither the machiavel's weapons nor his armour can be appropriated to their ends. Significantly, too, Shakespeare now blackens the machiavel more than he has ever done before. Iago has no such compunctuous visitings of nature as even Richard had, and no token repentance like Edmund's. He is a slave and a dog. The thought that he might be put to some good use, even in the second-best world of the political, is never entertained.

The public and political side of the grand theme, such as was handled in *Julius Caesar*, is brought back again in *Macbeth*. While it is given its full amplification, it is shown (as in *Troilus and Cressida*) subordinated to the spiritual transactions which take place in the private world. The public evil flows from the primary rebellion of Macbeth to his own nature. The public is included in the private and both are in relation to the benevolent metaphysical Nature. The machiavel, too, for the first time, is clearly related to this Nature. His generation is depicted in the degeneration of Macbeth. The root of machiavellism lies in a wrong choice. Macbeth is clearly aware of the great frame of Nature he is violating. He recognizes the unnaturalness of his deed, and is aware that the natural must ultimately be the most powerful. He gambles with Time, banking on the impossible chance that a series of short-term policies will defeat Nature's long-run restoration of her balance. He knows, however, he can be caught out in time as well as in 'the life to come'. The play ends with his defeat and with Nature's victory. Unlike *Othello*, *Macbeth* is a divine comedy.

The lucid synthesis of *King Lear* follows from a central re-adjustment which Shakespeare makes in his story. In all the other King-killing plays—with the possible exception of *Henry VI*—the King's death sets the stage. It is something, however, quite marginal to the main concerns. Now, however, Shakespeare takes the rightful King and transfers him from the wings into the centre of the stage. Furthermore, the slain Kings before had been figures of putative goodness—model Kings like Caesar or Hamlet's father or Duncan. King Lear, instead, is a rightful King, and a good King. But his nature is that more interesting thing—not the ideal but the human-natural, capable of corruption, error, rescue, and regeneration. King Lear is like Macbeth, only the scales in his case—after coming down on the wrong side—ultimately tilt the other way.

King Lear, then, omits nothing that is discoverable in *Macbeth* of relevance to displaying the grand theme. It gives a completer account than *Macbeth* by including what *Macbeth* omits. It follows on from *Macbeth* in its use of traditional theology. Each of the great figures of the tragic world is brought into relation with the Natures, to be elucidated and deepened.

Public and private are subordinated in the same way that they are in *Troilus and Cressida*. The initial lapse of the King's is in-

ward, and the upset in the outer world of the body politic follows as a consequence. The King is self-deceived. Like Brutus,
Hamlet, Troilus, and Othello, he cannot tell the truth from the
lie. The fault is his own, and no machiavel can be credited with
prime responsibility. With Lear more than any of the other
tragic heroes the sense of man, for good or ill, holding the key
to his own destiny is very strong.

The machiavel is brought into the tragic scheme, however.
Both as public danger and private devil, he is given full weight.
Shakespeare even extends the theology of Nature to accommo-
date the figure with a natural theology of his own. The machiavel is necessary to *King Lear* as it was to *Othello*. Once the Kingly
nature degenerates, machiavellism can usurp its place, storming
through the breach that self-rebellion has made. Goodness needs
always to beware of degeneration. Even when it has become
good again, it has still to contend with the machiavellism that
has grown strong by its original defection. Goodness needs a
community of goodness. And that is unlikely to be found in the
world. Lear therefore finds Cordelia dead in prison. While
taking over the 'Nature' theology of *Macbeth*, *King Lear* does
not forget the experience of *Othello*. It is the only other play in
the tragic period which can compare in poignancy with *Othello*.

The idea of a community of goodness being finally necessary
to resolve the human contradiction is carried even further. In
Lear's prayer, it is applied to human society and the equalitarian
dream of the Christian tradition revived. It is also, if we like,
suggested through the symbolism of Cordelia that only in an
ideal Jerusalem can the full fruit of goodness come to be. *King
Lear*, in any event, adds a new dimension to the tragic matter.
It is not merely a rearrangement of familiar material: it represents a new growth too.

The optimism of *Macbeth* is continued in regard to politics.
Edgar will defeat the machiavel, Nature will reassert itself in the
state. The good will not, however, be contaminated by any
truck with the machiavel's modes of action. Their crowning

strategy will be the strategy of patience: patience which is the faith that Nature is benevolent and also real, bound to vindicate herself both here and now as well as 'in the life to come'.

King Lear, in short, omits nothing that Shakespeare has discovered in his exploration of the natures, public and private, good and evil, true and seeming-true, since 1600. It's crowning achievement is to combine the 'pessimism' of *Othello* with the 'optimism' of *Macbeth* and fashion a play as rich and crowded and variegated as *Hamlet*. The optimism of *Macbeth* showed the victory of Nature. The pessimism of *Othello* showed the death of good Othello and immaculate Desdemona. The ending of *King Lear* shows the victory of Nature in the world of the common weal, but, in the private world, Cordelia's murder and Lear's heart-break: flinging us back thereby at one stroke to the Thunder again. For the Thunder is a part of the Lear universe: it may be the nature around the natures: the whatever-it-is that prompts such unanswerable queries as—What is the choice that has chosen choice?

CHAPTER V

KING LEAR

The key to Shakespeare's final handling of his theme consists, then, in this. Killing the King is put into a larger framework than Shakespeare has so far employed. Each of the main actors in the story is brought into relation with 'Nature'. By this each of them acquires an extra dimension. The theme itself is able to expand to its full extent, the parts are duly related, each issue is given its proper emphasis and proportion. At first killing the King was conceived as predominantly a public issue, a duel between a Henry and a Richard. The goodness of the King and the wickedness of the machiavel were unexamined axioms. By the time the first of the tragedies is written examination of the axioms has already begun. Shakespeare concentrates his attention on the King-slayer while the King himself remains a lay-figure. During this period the machiavel is seen as a special case of the hypocrite, and hypocrisy itself as something resulting from the precarious balance of our nature. *Hamlet* focuses on this radical duplicity, and its hero is appalled by man's capacity for self-rebellion, voluntary and involuntary. Shakespeare's interest remains centred on duplicity until *Macbeth*. With Macbeth the King-slayer is natural man, tempted from within and without to crime, changing through the consequences of crime into just such a devil as Richard Crookback was in the first place. The 'holy King', meanwhile, has continued to remain a lay-figure.

With *King Lear* the rightful King comes into his own. For the first time he is the focal-point of Shakespeare's interest. No longer a sovereign with a token-goodness, and as such made to stand for the ideal state of affairs, he is developed to full humanity. It is, in fact, because Lear is so much more a man than Julius Caesar or King Hamlet or Duncan that he is so much more effective than they are even as a symbol. For the King, in acquiring full humanity, never loses his original symbolic value.

Shakespeare now grounds his analysis of rebellion in the state on the analysis of defection in the 'little world' of individual man. He is helped in this all the time by the framework of the theology of Nature. As far back as *Troilus and Cressida* he has affirmed the primacy of the private sphere to the political: the latter is included in the former. Now he shows how both come under Nature. There are not two orders, but three.

It should be possible, therefore, through *King Lear* to explain what this 'King' is whose death, distress, or replacement Shakespeare has been so concerned about. To anticipate a conclusion, it is, I think, the fully traditional meaning of 'King' which Shakespeare arrives at. But Shakespeare returns to a tradition certainly older and possibly wiser than that of Tudor Despotism. To explain it fully will involve one more look at the notion of pattern in Nature which has already been touched on in connection with *The Ecclesiastical Polity*.

The pattern of the universe of created things, the pattern of man's own nature, and the pattern of his society, are similar structures. In each the whole is a unity requiring a due subordination of parts. The image whereby this hierarchy can best be comprehended is that of the pyramid. The universe, for example, is a structure which rises up through the diminishing multiplicities of the classes of created things to the One who is All. So in man: he is a hierarchical unity that grows to a point, that point the 'apex of the mind'—the part of him most fitted to be regarded as his highest and therefore his most real self. Man's society is inevitably similar. We rise upwards to the unity of that single man who is the King, passing through ranks that dwindle as to numbers but expand as to importance, and significance. The King finally stands for the whole. As the 'apex of the mind' is the essential self, the King is representative man. This view of the King as representative man underlies Gloster's cry when he sees the King a madman:

> O ruin'd piece of Nature, this great world
> Shall so wear out to nought.   (IV, vi.)

'Piece' here means 'masterpiece' not 'fragment', as it does for Cleopatra later:

> . . . yet t'imagine
> An *Anthony* were Natures peece, 'gainst Fancie.
> > (*Anthony and Cleopatra*, V, ii.)

To be representative man the King must embody, so to speak, the whole pattern. He must be the fullest human expression of the community that co-operates to maintain him. He must, besides, be representative in a more ultimate sense. He must express in act the King everyman is in potency. The authority of the King in the state will be unquestionable so long as the image of the King is retained in each subject, and so long as that same image is expressed by the King himself. The two things are interdependent. To threaten or overthrow the image in the individual is to threaten or overthrow it in the common weal. Collapse on one side will be followed by confusion on the other. The King thus stands for man at his best. And he stands for that which is best in man—the 'apex of the mind'. The 'marks of sovereignty', Lear will say, are 'knowledge and reason'. He is thinking of the 'apex of the mind', *ille igniculus luminis primi*: that whereby we know divinity, the common birthright which makes us all Kings.

In the state it is the King in everyman who submits to the King on the throne. The apparent paradox of such an equality entailing such a real subordination can be resolved in this way.— Everyman so submits himself because the King is in act what everyman is only in potency. The throne provides the only real opportunity for the nature of man to reach its full expression. No one besides the King can have the same scope, or power, or proper authority: for the authority will be the real right to rule of the good man who of all others has been given those conditions in which the seed of Kingliness can grow unhampered. Every other position in the hierarchy entails, of necessity, some diminution of the image of man: some falling short of its full expression. This being so subordination follows naturally. It is a necessity imposed on us by our inward nature, not a requirement from external compulsion. The lower must always submit to the higher. Every man's duty, therefore, is to play the part assigned him, to maintain the pattern that maintains the parts.

Everyman, at the same time, is not to be equated with his role. For he is also a King.—Shakespeare symbolizes this in *King Lear* in the otherwise inexplicable and arbitrary transformations through which Edgar's disguises run: beggarman, peasant, gentleman, national champion (a kind of Unknown Soldier), and finally the King. All are different roles. But in each role the same man is acting. Only the ideal order can be still. Imperfection, instability, or confusion will lay everyman open to the necessity of acting more parts than one, until the order is restored. Duplicity will be enjoined on him as a virtue.

To sum up, the idea of 'the King' has an inwardness in the traditional thought which for us has disappeared. The movement of thought is not from the political to the moral but from the moral to the political. It is because the individual is aware of pattern and its constituent parts in himself that he subscribes to it in the state. And in his little world everyman can be and should be a King. It is only so that he will discover and fulfil his right nature. The Kingly part in man is that whereby he is capable of being called 'the image of God', that which for Coverdale is 'natural honesty', for Hooker 'the light of Reason or Nature', for Bacon '*ille igniculus luminis primi quo divinitatem agnoscimus*'. It is this part of man (which like the King in the state can best stand for the whole) that all the other parts must co-operate with and be subordinate to. The inner order and the outer order thus interlock. Sin in the 'little world of man' is rebellion. Rebellion in the state is sin. The ordered nature of the individual cannot be fulfilled except in a properly ordered state. Disorder in the state will incur disorder in man. The parallelism is felt as more than analogy. The inner and outer worlds have organic connection through the relation in which each of them stands to their source. Both spheres take their order from the third sphere of Nature.

It is inevitable, therefore, that writers in the tradition Shakespeare is following should invariably bring public and private, political and moral, together. This has been called (rather abusively) 'anthropomorphism'. It is difficult to see how it could be anything else. For the state is an aspect of man, an extension from his inward nature. The parallelism is so close in the sixteenth century, in any event, that it is possible to talk of the state as a man and of man as a state. Two quotations from Erasmus's *Enchiridion*, abridged and translated by Coverdale in 1545, will serve to return us to the imagery of the sixteenth century which helps towards comprehending the imagery of *King Lear*. The first gives a picture of every man as a King:

Almighty God made man at the first of diverse parts, coupled with blessed concord; but the serpent, the enemy of peace, put them asunder again with unhappy discord, sowing the poison of dissension between them that were honestly agreed: insomuch that now neither the mind can rule the body without business, neither will the body obey without grudging. For whereas in man there should be such an order that like as in a prosperous commonalty, for avoiding of debate and strife, the wisest bear most rule, and the subjects obey their officers, this original decree of nature and first example of honesty notwithstanding, the order in man is so troubled, that the subjects will not obey the prince; yea, the corrupt affections and appetites of the flesh strive to be more master than reason itself; which unquiet affections whoso overcometh, the same liveth a blessed life, mounting up to celestial things, and as a King endowed with wisdom, willing and proposing to do nothing amiss, nothing against the judgment of reason, nothing inordinately, nothing frowardly, nothing corruptly.

The applicability of Coverdale to *King Lear* is immediate and obvious. Lear in Act I, scene i, is froward, and of a corrupted nature; he acts from inordinate wilfulness and against the judgment of reason as openly expressed to him through Kent. His sin leads him to give up the throne to the machiavels and this brings on discord in the state (the threatened war between the two daughters). The inner-outer parallelism works both ways. Having lost the throne Lear loses his reason. His madness on the heath is the anti-human counterpart in the 'little world of man' to the inhumanity of the official regime. The movement of Cordelia to restore the proper rule *ipso facto* makes Lear's return to sanity a possibility.

The second quotation explains the inward order of the three parts of man that have to be properly related:

Man, after the mind of Origen, is made of three parts. The first part is the flesh, wherein the malicious serpent through original trespass hath written the law of sin, whereby we be provoked into filthiness and coupled unto the devil if we be overcome. The second part is the spirit, wherein we represent the similitude of the nature of God; who after the eternal law of his own mind hath engraven therein the law of honesty, whereby we be knit unto God, and made one with him. The third part is the soul, partaken of the sensible wits and natural motions, which if she, forsaking the flesh, cleave unto the spirit, becometh spiritual; but if she follow the corrupt affections of the flesh, then joineth she herself unto an harlot, and is made one body with her that, being an evil, strange, flattering, foolish, and babbling, woman, breaketh her promise, and forsaketh the husband of her youth. Wherefore if we incline unto the spirit, it maketh us not only blessed, religious, obedient, kind, and merciful; but also teacheth us to desire celestial and necessary, pure, perfect, and godly things, to obey God rather than man, and though some affections be disguised with visors of virtue, yet not to be deceived with them. If we incline to the flesh it maketh us beasts, despisers of God, disobedient, unkind, and cruel; yea, and causeth us to desire delicate, pleasant, and filthy things. The rule of true goodness, therefore, is to lean as nigh unto the spirit, that for any good inclination or virtue we ascribe nothing to ourselves; that we do nothing for our own pleasure or advantage; that for observing of outward things we judge not ourselves better than other men; that we regard more our neighbour's necessity, and be readier to help them, than to keep men's traditions; that our love be chaste and spiritual.

The ground-plan of *King Lear* can be recognized in Coverdale's summary. Edmund and the Sisters are the Flesh: 'beasts, despisers of God, disobedient, unkind, and cruel'. The peculiar combination of 'delicate, pleasant, and filthy things' is found particularly in Goneril and Regan: in their gorgeousness and fastidiousness, mixing with the cat-like way they pursue Edmund and with the tigerish way they handle Gloster. Cordelia, of course, is the Spirit. She represents 'the law of honesty whereby we be knit unto God'. She is 'religious, obedient, kind, and merciful', yet she will 'obey God rather than men, and, though some affections be disguised with visors of virtue (e.g. the tact some critics wish she'd been endowed with, that agreeableness she might have had to humour her father as her sisters did) yet not . . . deceived by them'. Lear himself is the Soul, in a middle place between Edmund and Cordelia. As such he is capable of rejecting the Spirit. As such, too, of course, he is capable of being recalled and of turning again. The recipe for such regeneration, Coverdale suggests, is to 'regard more our neighbours' necessity'. Even this comes into the pattern of Shakespeare's play. Along with the patience he vainly strives to hold on to, Lear, before his madness, has the magnificent compassion of his prayer.

We can now see why it was necessary for Shakespeare to make the natural King himself the centre of the story that has to do with killing the King. To make any of the subsidiary figures the hero (as in *Macbeth*) prevents the whole pattern from developing. For the important thing about the King as a man is that he includes both sides of the argument in himself. He can be himself a rebel with Goneril and Regan, or he can maintain the order of Nature with Cordelia. Titular Kingship in itself is meaningless. No King has right authority unless the great image of Kingship is intact in him. The King good or bad, the state just or unjust, rebellion right or wrong, man himself a concord

or a discord: all depends on the transactions that take place between the King and Nature. For the King should be representative man, the expression of every man's 'natural honesty', and
as such the embodiment of the health of the state—a health of
'diverse parts coupled with blessed concord'.

The transactions between Lear and Nature we must now proceed to examine.

Throughout the play Lear's course describes a zigzag. Each
change of direction is a crucial response. Lear staggers from lapse
to recovery, through further relapse, to almost complete restoration, and finally to death. At the beginning of the play we are
watching an old man and his awkward family. At the end all
we can see is stricken Humanity holding murdered Nature in its
arms. No play grows so fast or so far as King Lear.

The motto for the first movement might well be Gloster's
summary: 'the King falls from the bias of Nature'. His first mistake and his ultimate recognition of the fault committed take
us up to the scenes on the heath.

At the outset Lear is an old man on the verge of 'dotage'. His
self-knowledge has never been strong, and infirmity of years has
made bad discrimination worse. Further, the decay of age ren-
ders him all the more liable to attacks of choler, and thereby to
the overclouding of reason. Lear meets his first opposition in
Cordelia. His abrupt recoil betrays itself immediately as wrongful. It is a violation of Nature all the more monstrous for invoking the very sanctities it violates:

> . . . thy truth then be thy dower:
> For by the sacred radiance of the sun,
> The mysteries of Hecate and the night:
> By all the operation of the orbs,
> From whom we do exist, and cease to be,
> Here I disclaim all my paternal care,
> Propinquity and property of blood,
> And as a stranger to my heart and me,
> Hold thee from this for ever. The barbarous Scythian,

> Or he that makes his generation messes
> To gorge his appetite, shall to my bosom
> Be as well neighbour'd, pitied, and reliev'd,
> As thou my sometime daughter.   (I, i.)

Among the Scythians parricide was accounted a virtue.

Lear goes with his hundred Knights to his eldest daughter's. Our next news of him is Goneril's account of how he is spending his holiday from Kingship:

> By day and night, he wrongs me, every hour
> He flashes into one gross crime, or other,
> That sets us all at odds: I'll not endure it;
> His knights grow riotous, and himself upbraids us
> On every trifle.   (I, iii.)

Old fools are babes again. In the first scene Lear's conduct was that of the neurotic—his neurosis one of old age and absolute power combined. Aware of the diminution of manhood involved in being a King—the deprivation of companionship, the absence of equal interchange, the impossibility of any education of the will or feelings among court flatterers or subservient hypocrites—he had resolved to give away his throne. To be less a King was to be more a man. This expression of neurosis was itself an attempt at a cure, but a cure self-prescribed, and as such likely to be dangerous. The prescription was actually mistaken. An aggravation of the disease was its only outcome. Lear on holiday is as egocentric as Lear partitioning the kingdom: and as childish. Such might be the modern version of what the Elizabethan medicals would explain in their own jargon of old age and a choleric humour. Lear out of office is, in any case, more testily obsessed with dignity and authority than he was when on the throne. This, the hunting and drinking and lechering apart, is not likely to be tolerated long. Lear meets his second opposition in the rebuff administered by Goneril.

The rebuff is sufficient to jolt Lear out of his rut of falsehood and by so much the nearer to the truth:

LEAR: Who is it that can tell me who I am?
FOOL: Lear's shadow.
LEAR: I would learn that, for by the marks of sovereignty, knowledge and reason, I should be false persuaded I had daughters. (I, iv.)

The phrase 'marks of sovereignty, knowledge and reason', as an echo of the traditional thought, has already been noted. Shakespeare overlays this thought here with his other theme of the truth and the seeming-truth. Lear is mistaken in his daughters, and mistaken in thinking that 'knowledge and reason' have been his guides. His distrust of what he calls in himself 'knowledge and reason' is the first sign so far that he is on the way to discovering real knowledge and the real reason. When the discovery is complete he will cease being a shadow and once more be himself.

The pause is only momentary. Lear's passion rises. Albany—always the 'moral fool'—calls out the advice from the devotionalists appropriate to the occasion: 'Pray sir be patient.' Patience is the only remedy in cases such as Lear's. Lear, however, flings into the angry venom of his outburst against Goneril. Patience is something he has yet to learn. But one thing he has learned. He can distinguish now between Cordelia and her sister:

> O most small fault,
> How ugly didst thou in Cordelia show?
> Which like an engine, wrench'd my frame of Nature
> From the fix'd place.   (I, iv.)

He knows, too, that he is fallen from 'the bias of Nature', and that the frame of Nature in him has been pulled away. It is to Nature that he prays:

> Hear Nature, hear dear Goddess, hear:
> Suspend thy purpose, if thou didst intend
> To make this creature fruitful:
> Into her womb convey sterility,
> Dry up in her the organs of increase.   (I, iv.)

The 'dear Goddess' is a different deity from Edmund's. Lear assumes she will automatically take sides with him against 'the degenerate bastard'.

So Lear goes to Regan. Letters meanwhile have reached her from her sister, and she is prepared. Lear meets vice wearing the visor of virtue. Regan uses the truth to further her lie. She sounds reasonable and solicitous:

> O sir, you are old,
> Nature in you stands on the very verge
> Of her confine: you should be rul'd, and led
> By some discretion, that discerns your state
> Better than you yourself: therefore I pray you,
> That to our sister you do make return,
> Say you have wrong'd her.   (II, ii.)

Rather than apologize Lear would prefer mere 'raiment, bed and food' in Regan's castle:

> Dear daughter, I confess that I am old;
> Age is unnecessary: on my knees I beg,
> That you'll vouchsafe me raiment, bed, and food.
>   (II, ii.)

Lear's education in humility is proceeding apace: 'Like as prosperity shutteth and blindeth the eyes of men, even so doth adversity and trouble open them.' He is mistaken enough, still, however, to believe that Regan is different from Goneril:

> Thy tender-hefted Nature shall not give
> Thee o'er to harshness . . .
>   . . . Thou better know'st
> The offices of Nature, bond of childhood,
> Effects of courtesy, dues of gratitude.   (II, ii.)

Too late, Lear understands what Cordelia meant by 'bond' and he uses the word in her sense. His outbursts of passion alternate with motions in the direction of Spirit and away from Flesh.

In an effort towards amendment of life he will even add patience to humility. When Goneril has joined Regan, and the cross-bidding in retrenchments is just beginning, he is willing to go a long way in compliance.

But I'll not chide thee,
Let shame come when it will, I do not call it,
I do not bid the Thunder-bearer shoot,
Nor tell tales of thee to high-judging Jove,
Mend when thou canst, be better at thy leisure,
I can be patient, I can stay with Regan,
I and my hundred Knights.   (II, ii.)

The patience he has learned, of course, is not perfect. It depends
on his striking the bargain on those favourable terms he takes
for granted. And the daughters are just beginning their inverted
bids. By the time they are finished patience has once more given
way to passion:

GONERIL: Hear me, my Lord:
          What need you five and twenty? Ten? or five?
          To follow in a house, where twice so many
          Have a command to tend you?
REGAN: What need one?
LEAR: O reason not the need: our basest beggars
          Are in the poorest things superfluous,
          Allow not Nature, more than Nature needs:
          Man's life is cheap as beasts. Thou art a Lady;
          If only to go warm were gorgeous,
          Why Nature needs not what thou gorgeous wear'st,
          Which scarcely keeps thee warm, but for true need,
          You Heavens, give me that patience, patience I need,
          You see me here, you Gods, a poor old man,
          As full of grief as age, wretched in both,
          If it be you that stir these daughters' hearts
          Against their father, fool me not so much
          To bear it tamely: touch me with noble anger,
          And let not woman's weapons, water-drops,
          Stain my man's cheeks. No you unnatural hags
          I will have such revenges on you both,
          That all the world shall—I will do such things,
          What they are yet, I know not, but they shall be
          The terrors of the earth! You think I'll weep,
          No, I'll not weep. I have full cause for weeping.
                                        Storm and Tempest.

But this heart shall break into a hundred thousand flaws
Or ere I'll weep. O fool, I shall go mad.   (II, ii.)

The speech summarizes and concludes the first phase. Lear begins
with the distinction between man's animal needs and his natural
requirements. He insists on the ascending gradation of Nature.
He points to the 'nature' which man takes from society, to
which beasts cannot aspire. Simultaneously he aims side-blows
at that actual society which affronts Nature's equity—the society
that houses simultaneously the 'basest beggar' and the 'gorgeous'
queens. Then follows the recognition of his real need, patience;
the humble and abject confession of helplessness; the recognition
that adversity comes from God: 'and although trouble and afflic-
tion riseth and springeth often times by the wickedness of enemies, and through the instigation of the devil, or else by some
other means; yet ought we never to imagine that it cometh by
fortune or chance, without the permission, sufferance, deter-
mination, and will of God'. But Lear's patience is fitful, and his
charity imperfect. Willing to suppose that the adversity is
stirred up by God, he is unwilling to forgive the enemies who
are God's instruments. He returns once more to the mood of the
first scene. There he took upon himself to be God the rewarder
of merits. Now he will be God the avenger of iniquities.

As he speaks the Thunder breaks in on his tirade. It may be in
sympathy with Lear's threats. It may be the ally of the pelican
daughters, adding its own quota of cruelty to theirs. The Thunder brings a new 'nature' on to the stage. With its appearance a
fresh movement begins.

In Act III 'the wound becomes greater than what it cuts'. This
is so because the situation now grows so far and so fast that the
spectator seems to be included in it along with Lear. It is not
Lear's mind only that is gashed and riven down to its root. It is
ours also. It is not only Lear's local world that is torn open, it is
ours, too. We are no longer spectators of *this* man in *those*

circumstances. We occupy the same heath as Lear and are fellow
agents and patients.

Sympathy with Lear's sufferings will not explain this turn.
Nor is it a case of daydream identification with a hero. What
happens is that the root of the mind is reached and activated,
made to share in the spectator's hold on the meaning of what is
taking place before his eyes. For Shakespeare does not give us
meaning as an 'attitude to life'. He presents us with a choice, as
Spenser did in his pictures of the Goddess. Before we can have
the meaning, we must make the choice. And choice is the root
of mind.

The agent responsible for this radical transformation is the
Thunder. The Thunder says nothing. Or it says the same thing
all the time, and that thing unintelligible. Yet each person submitted to it acts as though it were thoroughly understood. But
as each responds according to his lights, it is many different
things it must be saying. Kent's reaction is to cry:

> Such sheets of fire, such burst of horrid thunder,
> Such groans of roaring wind, and rain, I never
> Remember to have heard. Man's Nature cannot carry
> Th' affliction, nor the fear. (III, ii.)

and later:

> Good, my lord, enter:
> The tyranny of the open night's too rough
> For Nature to endure. (III, iv.)

The reactions of the Fool and Lear differ from this and from
each other:

LEAR: You sulphurous and thought-executing fires,
　　　Vaunt-couriers of oak-cleaving thunderbolts,
　　　Singe my white head. And thou all-shaking thunder
　　　Strike flat the thick rotundity o' th' world,
　　　Crack Nature's moulds, all germens spill at once
　　　That makes ingrateful man.

FOOL: O nuncle, Court holy-water in a dry house, is better than this
　　　rain-water out o' door. Good nuncle, in, ask thy daughter's blessing;
　　　here's a night pities neither wise men, nor fools.

LEAR: Rumble thy bellyful: spit fire, spout rain:
    Nor rain, wind, thunder, fire are my daughters;
    I tax not you, you elements, with unkindness.
    I never gave you Kingdom, call'd you children;
    You owe me no subscription. Then let fall
    Your horrible pleasure. Here I stand your slave,
    A poor, infirm, weak, and despis'd old man:
    But yet I call you servile ministers,
    That will with two pernicious daughters join
    Your high-engender'd battles, 'gainst a head
    So old, and white as this. O, ho! 'tis foul.

FOOL: He that has a house to put's head in, has a good head-piece:
    The codpiece that will house,
    Before the head has any;
    The head, and he shall louse:
    So beggars marry many.
    The man that makes his toe,
    What he his heart should make,
    Shall of a corn cry woe,
    And turn his sleep to wake.
    For there was never yet fair woman but she made mouths in a
      glass.

Enter Kent.

LEAR: No, I will be the pattern of all patience,
    I will say nothing.

KENT: Who's there?

FOOL: Marry here's Grace, and a codpiece, that's a wise man, and a
    fool. . . .

LEAR: Let the great Gods
    That keep this dreadful pudder o'er our heads,
    Find out their enemies now. Tremble thou wretch
    That hast within thee undivulged crimes
    Unwhipp'd of Justice. . . .
        . . . I am a man
    More sinn'd against, than sinning.   (III, ii.)

Lear now detaches himself from the group of those whom up to
this point we have regarded as his protectors. He becomes different in stature from them. He is the King again. We are soon to
see Lear as a shattered ruin of humanity. Meanwhile we are

given this view of him as the symbol for humanity's greatness and endurability. Lear has rejected Cordelia and recoiled from Goneril and Regan. Between horror of the Flesh and despair of the Spirit the soul might be expected to stand only on the bridge of self-pity. There is actually a trace of something that resembles self-pity. But it is only momentary. Even when Lear points to himself as 'a poor old man', the manner of it is factual and impersonal. He is mainly appalled at a general injustice his particular case exemplifies. For the rest, self-pity cannot last under the opposite stresses of indignation and remorse, the 'to-and-fro conflicting wind and rain'.

On the heath, then, there is only Lear who will measure himself against the Thunder.

What the Thunder is we can no more learn from Lear's reactions than from those of anyone else. Lear's attitude is profoundly ambivalent. The Thunder is first his agent. It is executing the King's desires in annihilating the corrupted world of man. Again, Lear is not the Thunder's master, but it's slave:

> . . . a poor, infirm, weak and despis'd old man.

His indignation is merely a shadow of the Thunder's. Then, again, the Thunder is the 'servile minister' of his daughters, neither just nor great, wreaking its spite on a powerless victim. Lear exhausts himself in his effort to comprehend it, and falls back on 'saying nothing':

> No, I will be the pattern of all patience: I will say nothing.

Finally the Thunder becomes merely the sign of some vague disturbance among 'the great gods'. Let these search out all the hidden wickedness of the earth. Lear himself will be free from their attentions:

> Close pent-up guilts
> Rive your concealing continents, and cry
> These dreadful summoners grace. I am a man
> More sinned against than sinning.

This is the reversal of the judgment we have been making on

Lear in the first two Acts. It is equally amazing that Lear should make it so confidently on his own behalf, and that we should be prepared to entertain it. That we should, we can repeat, is not an effect of the sympathy we have for an old man suffering. It results from the Thunder and the question the Thunder forces up: what relation is there between the moral world of man and its containing universe?

The Thunder is a profoundly ambiguous creature. An easy evasion is to understand it as 'pathetic fallacy', or to think of it as the romantic 'Nature', or physical Nature, or Hardy's Nature, or Darwin's. There is no doubt that critics have variously interpreted the play as they have variously interpreted the Thunder which dominates Act III.

The clue to Shakespeare's meaning is to be sought, I think, as far back as *Julius Caesar* where the nature of Thunder is first debated. In *King Lear* as in *Julius Caesar* the Thunder has metaphysical status. It is the super-natural and the super-rational and the super-human. It belongs not only with the Thunder in *Julius Caesar*, but with the ambiguous ghost in *Hamlet*, the delphic Cassandra of *Troilus and Cressida*, the doubtful witches of *Macbeth*. To say this, of course, is in itself to say little enough. A little more can possibly be added.

In each of these cases a question is put not only to man's will but to his reason: is the one free and is the other reliable? The mere possibility of there being a question here at all serves to suggest a frame wider than anything even our wisest and noblest use of reason and will can find satisfaction in. In Lear, it suggests a frame wider even than that which stretches between Cordelia and Edmund. *King Lear*, we have tried to suggest, has in Cordelia its own beatific knowledge of order. Cordelia is Shakespeare's Beatrice. To put even Cordelia in the framework of Thunder is an enormous achievement. It gives Shakespeare an inclusiveness which even Dante falls short of.

The suggestion is sufficient, as it were, to make judgment prepare to swing round on to a fresh axis. Choice is left completely free. Lear instead of an aberrant father might well be 'more sinned against than sinning.' For the radical ambiguity of the Thunder cannot be dismissed by the application of an order-disorder theory. The Thunder, as Lear reacts to it, might itself be an order and not a chaos: an order in comparison with which our smaller orders of degree and gradation are only broken fragments.

The Thunder, then, in my view, presents us with a choice. Our reaction to it (whereby alone we can know it) must be a choice. Shakespeare makes man's will a component part of man's knowledge, man's reason something man must make. By the mere presence of Thunder we are forced to shed our habitual moralities. Tragedy effects its purgation. The mind is cleansed. We are called upon to choose again. After such a purge Cordelia will not be put on one side for anything inferior. But the return to her—like Lear's return—will be choice not chance.

Under Thunder, the miracle of Lear's rehabilitation is achieved. He can now make man's most dignified and deeply felt demand —the demand that his universe shall be a just one. And Lear is admitted to be a fit vehicle for the demand. He symbolizes man's inherent nobility, what the *Enchiridion* called 'natural honesty'. And the growth in stature is not yet finished. There is a last enlarging and sweetening of Lear to take place before he is made mad.

This last and grandest act of his sanity is the prayer:

> I'll pray, and then I'll sleep.
> Poor naked wretches, wheresoe'er you are
> That bide the pelting of this pitiless storm,
> How shall your houseless heads, and unfed sides,
> Your loop'd and window'd raggedness defend you
> From seasons such as these? O I have ta'en
> Too little care of this: take physic, pomp,
> Expose thyself to feel what wretches feel,
> That thou mayst shake the superflux to them,
> And show the heavens more just.   (III, iv.)

The prayer, in the first place, is not a chance impulse of Shakespeare's: it is carefully placed in a deliberate design. Second, this placing shows that Shakespeare is following the traditional schema of spiritual regeneration laid down in the devotionalists. Third, it is the sentiment of Christian 'communism' which it expresses. Fourth, this 'communism' itself forms part of a long tradition still active in the sixteenth century, and ready to emerge into the world of seventeenth-century politics whenever the opportunity offers.

The deliberateness of the prayer can be gathered from the fact that Gloster repeats it at a similar stage in a similar process of regeneration:

> Here take this purse, you whom the heavens' plagues
> Have humbled to all strokes: that I am wretched
> Makes thee happier: Heavens deal so still:
> Let the superfluous, and lust-dieted man,
> That slaves yon ordinance, that will not see
> Because he does not feel, feel your power quickly:
> So distribution should undo excess,
> And each man have enough.   (IV, i.)

In each case the prayers indicate returning spiritual health. Lear's hold on this state is soon to be lost. The mood, however, is not in itself an idle one. To humility and patience, through the experience of adversity, charity has been added: 'The rule of true goodness, therefore, is to lean as nigh unto the spirit, that for any good inclination or virtue we ascribe nothing to ourselves; that we do nothing for our own pleasure or advantage; that for observing of outward things we judge not ourselves better than other men, that we regard more our neighbour's necessity, and be readier to help them, than to keep men's traditions.' Charity, repentance, a renewed will to amendment, an awareness of his neighbours accompanying the new awareness of himself, the falling away of original egocentricity, of anger, revenge, impatience with the Heavens—the prayer shows Lear's mind settling itself in its proper frame. The true bias has been found again.

The third point of the prayer's 'communism' has not been made much of by commentators. Yet it is a Christian levelling of society—the logical and full expression of charity—which is pointed to. The 'superflux' of the 'superfluous' man is all that which he has in excess of his needs, not merely those crumbs which he can afford to do without. Such a distribution as will undo excess will obviously lead to an equalitarian society. Thus, Lear's new-found private goodness requires a community of goodness to relate itself to. And this new society will be different from that over which Lear ruled originally. It will also be different from the society of his daughters which has ejected him.

The primitive communism of the prayer comes, I think, both from Shakespeare's reaction to 'the times' and from the Christian tradition. In Beghards, Fraticelli, and Lollards, equalitarian sentiments had been a permanent feature of the medieval underworld. The medieval mood broke out violently in the Anabaptists. After the rising of the 'Zwickau Prophets' in 1525, a company of these migrated to England. Two of their tenets were: that there must be a visible Kingdom of Christ on earth; that in this Kingdom all must be equal and enjoy community of goods. The rising after 1525 seemed even more dangerous. In 1534, under a new leader, theocracy was established at Munster. A tailor of Leyden was crowned King of the New Jerusalem; an attempt made to take Amsterdam itself and incorporate it in the new dispensation. Throughout the sixteenth century the Anabaptists are constantly being denounced by the more orthodox Reformers. They are coupled with Manichees in the theological denunciations. In England the last burnings of Anabaptist refugees took place in 1577. But, in a milder and modified form, Anabaptism continued—preaching against capital punishment and the use of weapons, and practising re-baptism. Splinter parties of religious eccentrics seem to have kept the extremer traditions alive. The Family of Love of Messianic Henry Nicolas (*Homo Novus*) is proclaimed against in 1580. The Familists, Seekers and Ranters come fully into their own in the early seventeenth century. Edward Wightman (a Seeker who suffered from Messianic delusions) was the last man to be burned for heresy in England. William Laud attended his trial in 1611. With the Levellers and Diggers, the trickle then becomes a stream; in Winstanley, singularly sweet and clear. It runs on, maybe underground, to reappear undoubtedly in Blake: a heresy that has passed through Lear's prayer on the Heath and issued finally into 'Songs af Experience'.

Zwickau prophets, Diggers, Winstanley and Blake are an unusually hectic company to associate with Shakespeare. The vital and continuous ferment this sequence points to, however, is a necessary aspect of 'the times' to which Shakespeare was reacting, to which he was giving in his drama proper form and pressure. A less hectic pedigree for the prayer could easily be provided. Jack Cade of *Henry VI* indicates Shakespeare's acquaintance with the notions of revolt and the equality of man. There was, further, John Ball's sermon in Froissart to read: 'Ah, ye good people, the matters goeth not well to pass in England, nor shall do till everything be common, and that there be no villeins nor gentlemen, but that we be all together, and that the lords be no greater masters than we be.' Growing out of the main tradition, there was also the communistic fancy of More's *Utopia*. There is, finally, the homilist's arraignment of pomp from the fourteenth-century sermon book: evidence, as Professor Owst suggests, of how far the popular preacher could go in social iconoclasm. The Poor Man's case against the rich and powerful at the last judgment is as moving as Lear's:

We hungered and thirsted and were afflicted with cold and nakedness. And those robbers yonder gave not our goods to us when we were in want, neither did they feed or clothe us out of them. But their hounds and horses and apes, the rich, the powerful, the abounding, the gluttons, the drunkards and the prostitutes they fed and clothed with them, and allowed us to languish in want. . . . O just God, mighty judge, the game was not fairly divided between them and us. Their satiety was our famine; their merriment was our wretchedness; their jousts and tournaments were our torments, because with our oats and at our expense they did these things.

Christian levelling was then a potential political factor throughout the sixteenth and seventeenth centuries; it had been a sentiment implicit in the main stream of the Christian tradition; it could be at any time a possibility from 'charity' working in the individual soul. Shakespeare would come upon some of its expressions in his source-books and learn something of Anabaptism as he learned something of machiavellism from an indignant and widespread counter-campaign.

All these considerations have a certain force in leading to a reassessment of the prayer in relation to Shakespeare's work. The strongest argument for its central significance, however, is the evidence from Shakespeare's own development. Shakespeare's own vision after *Othello* leads him to realize that private goodness can only be permanent in a society of goodness. *King Lear* has the pure tragedy of *Othello* just because its regenerate Lear and incorruptible Cordelia are made the victims, in the end, not of a 'tragic fault', but of the evil co-present with them in the human universe. As well as being Shakespeare's reaction to Christian thought, Lear's prayer is the logical outcome of Shakespeare's own achieved insights, the wisdom the tragic period establishes in him intrinsically.

The rest of Lear's course through the play is soon told, and its general significance in terms of the Natures we have already hinted at. Lear meets Poor Tom, goes mad, is restored and finally dies.

The basic pattern of *King Lear* is made up of immensely strong contrasts. Lear's madness is juxtaposed to the Prayer immediately—this is contrast internal to a single character. Lear comes face to face with Poor Tom: this is contrast as between characters.

Poor Tom is a highly appropriate congeries of meanings. He is a human bankrupt, haunted by the fiends of past and now meaningless lusts, cast out from society, shut off from the spirit, incapable of regeneration. He personifies the twin symbols of the Fool's verse. He is the Courtier-Beggarman who of his corn cries woe:

A servingman! Proud in heart, and minde; that curl'd my hair, wore gloves in my cap; serv'd the lust of my Mistress' heart, and did the act of darkness with her. Swore as many oaths, as I spake words, and broke them in the sweet face of Heaven. One, that slept in the contriving of lust, and wak'd to do it. Wine lov'd I dearly, dice early; and in woman, out-paramour'd the Turk. False of heart, light of ear, bloody of hand; hog in sloth, fox in stealth, wolf in greediness, dog in madness, lion in prey. Let not the creaking of shoes, nor the rustling of silks, betray thy poor heart to woman. Keep thy foot out of brothels, thy hand out of plackets, thy pen from lenders' books, and defy the foul Fiend. (III, iv.)

As in the Fool's verse, the imagery of the corrupt affections intertwines with the imagery of corrupt society. Poor Tom is a scarlet sinner, and also a landed gentleman who ran into debt.— All the time, of course, Poor Tom is Edgar in the first of his disguises: a simular of virtue. Natural goodness will rive its concealing continent if only we are patient. For Edgar is the machiavel of patience, of ripeness, of God's ultimate revenges. In the natural sphere there is apparently a duplicity of virtue. Even charity is gashed with guilt; compassion itself is the sign of a breach in nature; all have offended and have need of the glory of God. There is similarly, within the limits of a world that includes the evil machiavel, a virtue of duplicity. The pleated cunning of the sisters will be outmatched by this virtue that wears the visor of vice. Edgar, therefore, slips from role to role. Poor Tom is followed by the peasant, the peasant by the gentleman, the gentleman by the shining champion, until finally Edgar is himself again, and, with Kent, is made King of England. The roles in their sequence suggest two things: the singleness of the essential nature of man at every level and in every social function; second, the ability of the seed of 'natural honesty' to quicken in the Beggarman and transform the beggarman into a King. Edgar at the end of the play is the national champion of the Falconbridge tradition; the Kingly nature considered as inherent in the stuff of valiant humanity rather than in any dynastic title to a throne.

For Lear, of course, whom we have just in the Prayer scene accepted as the image of man's grandeur and dignity, the apparition before him is 'the thing itself'. Shakespeare here plays on his theme of the truth and the seeming truth to achieve even a new richness of effect. It is not Edgar, but Edgar's pretence that is taken to be the final summary of man's nature: 'unaccommodated man, is no more but such a poor, bare, forked animal as thou art'. The two contrasted views of nature are thus brought on to the stage together. It is the effect that Sir J. Davies tries in a small way in *Nosce Teipsum*:

> And to conclude, I know myself a man,
> Which is a proud and yet a wretched thing.

Lear's madness has three aspects. As has already been suggested, it is the counterpart in the 'little world' of the inhumanity of the state ruled over by the machiavels. Secondly it is to be regarded as a mercy: 'Better I were distract', Gloster says,

> So should my thoughts be sever'd from my griefs,
> And woes by wrong imaginations lose
> The knowledge of themselves.   (IV, vi.)

Lear in his madness cannot feel. He is spared the real suffering of remorse or the real agony of compassion. Thirdly, it shows the shattering of the pattern of reason and nature. Lear mad exemplifies the handy-dandy which the Fool's verse plays with. In his case, however, the wheel on which he is bound is 'a wheel of fire'. It is a ledge like the Fool's he stands on. On one hand is the foul pit of evil, on the other the impossible cliff of perfection: a horror of the flesh, and a despair of the spirit. Justice, Authority, the Kingly nature, patience, hypocrisy—each of the great themes is touched upon, but all of them twisted awry. The tree of integrated humanity shivers and disbranches. The imagery in which the revulsion expresses itself recalls *Hamlet*. There is the same nausea and the same spreading paralysis of distrust. The madness negates all those positive values integrated into the figure of Cordelia. Its imagery is perversely sexual. Its central symbol is a counter-Cordelia:

LEAR: Behold yond simpering dame, whose face between her forks presages snow; that minces virtue, and does shake the head to hear of pleasure's name. The fitchew nor the soiled horse goes to't with a more riotous appetite. Down from the waist they are Centaurs, though women all above: but to the girdle do the Gods inherit, beneath is all the Fiends. There's hell, there's darkness, there is the sulphurous pit; burning, scalding, stench, consumption: fie, fie, fie; pah, pah: give me an ounce of civet; good apothecary, sweeten my imagination: there's money for thee.
GLOSTER: O let me kiss that hand.
LEAR: Let me wipe it first, it smells of mortality.
GLOSTER: O ruin'd piece of Nature, this great world
      Shall so wear out to nought.   (IV, vi.)

Woman's nature demonstrates the mechanical handy-dandy. Fissured humanity plays a game in which both the worlds suffer. Justice is the same:

Change places, and handy-dandy, which is the Justice, which is the thief?   (IV, vi.)

The spiritual coherence of the prayer is disintegrated. The Pauline 'All have offended' becomes Lear's 'None does offend, none, I say none'. Charity spills over and loses all form or meaning. Its perfectionism negates itself: such charity must necessarily leave things as it found them:

      Then comes the time, who lives to see't,
      That going shall be us'd with feet.   (III, ii.)

For essential humanity and the preservation of the shape and pattern both of man and his society there is substituted the insane passion to destroy.

The swiftest and most startling conjunction of opposites in all

Lear's speeches is that where he plays the part, first, of preacher
on the text of 'Patience', then suddenly breaks off his sermon to
become the bloody-minded and machiavellian killer:

> If thou wilt weep my fortunes, take my eyes.
> I know thee well enough, thy name is Gloster:
> Thou must be patient; we came crying hither:
> Thou know'st the first time that we smell the air
> We wawl, and cry. I will preach to thee: Marke . . .
> When we are born, we cry that we are come
> To this great stage of fools. This' a good block:
> It were a delicate stratagem to shoe
> A troop of horse with felt: I'll put't in proof,
> And when I have stol'n upon these son-in-Laws,
> Then Kill, kill, kill, kill, kill, kill   (IV, vi.)

It is just at this juncture that word gets through from Cordelia.
Lear runs off mad. We hear the Gentleman's words:

> Thou hast a daughter
> Who redeemes Nature from the generall curse
> Which twain have brought her to.   (IV, vi.)

Lear's rejection of Cordelia led to his madness, and caused
society to change from a comfort to a curse. When Cordelia
finds him again the process is reversed, both for Lear and for the
common weal.

Lear is found by Cordelia on the eve of the battle with Goneril,
Regan, and Edmund. In that battle Cordelia is defeated and both
she and Lear are taken prisoners. By now the issues centred in
'character' are exhausted. The fall from Nature and the redemption of Nature in the private world have reached a conclusion.
There remain the issues of the redemption of the state (the working out of which is left to Edgar, Cordelia's counterpart in the
sub-plot) and the metaphysics of Thunder: is the death of Cordelia the great world of Nature wearing out to nought, or is it
just plain fact as against Cordelia's transcendent truth? These
issues go beyond the 'little world' of man. The story now
emerges in its own right as the sole agent capable of carrying all

the play's related meanings to their end. And it seems that not only now but all along the bare contour of the story has been expressing the play's most inward meanings. The meaning we arrive at after long search is that which all along has lain most obviously on the surface. The outline of the story itself has the force of symbol. The story is a parable.

But before the play ends Lear is given one more great speech. In its way the speech is as prophetic as the prayer. Just as the prayer opens out one vista into the historical future (the future of western man in his society) this speech opens another. The story comments ironically on the speech; it points to the continuing possibility of concentration camp, and to the continuing impossibility of goodness insulating itself against the world in any kind of virtuous ivory tower. Lear is clinging to Cordelia. His goodness is convalescent. While she would move with level self-possession to meet 'these sisters and these daughters' Lear shrinks from the encounter:

LEAR: No, no, no, no; come let's away to prison,
We two alone will sing like birds i' th' cage:
When thou dost ask me blessing, I'll kneel down
And ask of thee forgiveness: so we'll live,
And pray, and sing, and tell old tales, and laugh
At gilded butterflies: and hear (poor rogues)
Talke of Court news, and we'll talk with them too,
Who loses, and who wins; who's in, who's out;
And take upon's the mystery of things,
As if we were God's spies: and we'll wear out
In a wall'd prison, packs and sects of great ones,
That ebb and flow by th' moon.

BASTARD: Take them away.

LEAR: Upon such sacrifices, my Cordelia,
The Gods themselves throw Incense. Have I caught thee?
He that parts us, shall bring a brand from Heaven
And fire us hence, like foxes: wipe thine eyes,
The good-years shall devour them, flesh and fell,
Ere they shall make us weep:
We'll see 'em starve first: come.   (V, iii.)

Lear looks forward to mutual forgiveness in a walled prison.
These are the only terms the corrupt world will allow to goodness. Lear imagines such an arrangement will even be regarded
as an indefinitely prolongable *modus vivendi*. The good will be
'foxes' again. Their strategy will be a cunning superior to the fox-
ship of the machiavels. Or they will be God's spies in the enemy
courts of the great ones. By patience they will wear out the
packs and sects that ebb and flow by the moon.

The story presses on to a conclusion contrary to Lear's imagin-
ings. Cordelia is strangled in her cell. The last scene shows us
Lear—mad again—with his dead daughter:

> And my poor fool is hang'd: no, no, no life?
> Why should a dog, a horse, a rat have life,
> And thou no breath at all? Thou'lt come no more,
> Never, never, never, never, never.   (V, iii.)

The ending of the play returns us to the Thunder, and to the
choice.

Lear's prophecy concerning Cordelia is again fulfilled, this
time in Shakespeare's art. He is unable to write another play like
King Lear. *Timon* is an unnatural fantasy, a *King Lear* without
Cordelia. The last plays seem to belong to the mood of Lear's
convalescence. Shakespeare weaves his stories round a theme
other than 'Killing the King'. In these stories Lear and Cordelia
find each other again and live happily ever after.

SUMMARY

The universal work 'grows up from the deeps of Nature, through the noble sincere soul who is a voice of Nature'. We have tried to show that 'the deeps of Nature' underlying Shakespeare's work include the nature of the society and 'the times' into which Shakespeare was born. *King Lear* elucidates the human plight at a particular phase in its historical unfolding. We have also tried to show, besides this, how *King Lear* explains Shakespeare's own development. It is the culmination of a process of growth which began in the first Chronicle plays. It fulfils and, it would seem, it concludes that growth. If this is right it should be possible therefore to table the definite conclusions Shakespeare reaches.

First, for the conclusion reached on that question the Tudors put before all others—the right to rebel. Shakespeare's thought runs through three stages. The first stage is completed in his handling of Richard Crookback, the arch-rebel and devil. Rebellion against the legitimate and (above all) the pious King is wrong. Only such a monster as Richard, foe to God and Man, would attempt it. The second stage begins with *King John*. Rebellion now, even against a wrongful usurper, is never justifiable. Shakespeare adopts the official Tudor ideology preserved for us in the Homilies. The third stage begins with *Julius Caesar*. Professor Dover Wilson is right, I think, in regarding 1599 as a Shakespearian climacteric. The year of Essex's rebellion marks a decisive change of direction in Shakespeare's development.

One sign (maybe resulting from the proven danger of any open reference to contemporary affairs) is the switch from English history to the camouflage of Roman, Danish, Scottish, Trojan, or Ancient British chronicle matter. Shakespeare's art, however, is not unduly tongue-tied by the Lord Chamberlain's authority. The new plays continue to handle the old theme, but with a radical change of attitude on the central issue. Shakespeare now justifies tyrannicide. Successive kings are killed for a succession of reasons. In this the tragedies appear to revert to the orthodox attitude of the earliest Chronicles. The attitudes, however, are not identical. Whereas the *Henry VI* tetralogy could be countenanced by the reigning house because Henry Tudor's own rebellion to end rebellion constituted the *grand finale*, the tragedies make no such concession. Their conclusion is plain and unqualified. It is right to rebel against usurper or tyrant.

King Lear, of course, written in 1606, belongs to the first years of James's reign. By this time the Elizabethan playwright, like the ex-Elizabethan Parliament, can come out into more open opposition. James may claim nothing that Elizabeth had not claimed before him. Neither Parliament nor playwright, however, will concede to the Stuart what they did to Elizabeth Tudor. So Nicholas Breton is able to write a sketch of the *Unworthy King* in 1614, such as would have been highly injudicious ten years before that time:

An unworthy King is the usurper of power, where tyranny in authority loseth the glory of majesty, while the fear of terror frighteneth love from obedience. . . . He knows no God, but makes an idol of Nature, and useth reason, but to the ruin of sense. His care is but his will, his pleasure but his ease, his exercise but sin, and his delight but inhuman. His heaven is his pleasure and his gold is his god.

Nicholas Breton's unworthy king is Macbeth and Edmund combined, with a suggestion of Volpone thrown in at the end for good measure. It seems to have been easier in James's reign to speak one's mind.

The unworthy king 'knows no God, but makes an idol of

Nature, and useth reason, but to the ruin of sense'. It is significant that the ideas come up, not singly, but in groups. Shakespeare's thought on Rebellion is not intrinsically important. Rebellion is only one of a family of related issues. A proper opinion on this matter indicates right orientation generally. And right orientation was deemed necessary for both mental and social stability.

Elizabeth's doctrine of rebellion represented the renaissance despot's incursion into the territory of theology proper. It adjusted the traditional teaching to the requirements of the authoritarian prince. During the sixteenth century the clergy were dispossessed, the monastery lands shared out among a new aristocracy, government was centralized, and a new King's household created: administrators with vested interests in the new order. The control of the parish pulpit, and through that of the only means of propaganda, completed the monolith of the nation state. Other ideas group themselves inevitably with the idea of Rebellion because the doctrine of rebellion itself merely symptomatized important changes over a wide field. The sixteenth century produced new incidences of stress in the whole community of the traditional opinions. Rebellion, for example, was connected with order. Along with order, the ideas of Reason, Nature, and God were also affected.

In Part I we tried to show how *King Lear* reflects the alternative readings of man's position in regard to God and his neighbour which were current at the turn of the century. The main choice lay between the dead mechanical Nature of the infidel politician and the normative moral Nature of the worthy King; between the Lion-headed Goddess and the Goddess, God's handmaid, whose face was that of a beautiful woman; between the Nature of Edmund and the Nature of Cordelia; that of Hobbes and that of Hooker. Shakespeare was born at a time when the afterglow of the Middle Ages was still casting strong lights and vivid shadows. But Galileo, too, was born in 1564. The ferment of a new world was at work.

Shakespeare's clearest symbolization of 'the times' is his treatment of what we called the New Man. Again three stages are discernible in his thought.

In the first tetralogy the New Man was also the diabolical machiavel. Opposite him ranged the effete and holy King—'pity, fear, and love'. At the beginning of his investigation Shakespeare works to the formula of Tudor propaganda. The rebel is a devil and Henry Tudor restores rightness as well as legitimacy. In the machiavel, however, Shakespeare dramatizes the chief duplicity of his century. The centre no longer holds, things inseparate divide more wider than the sky and earth, the state is a business run by the politician, and the behaviour of the statist can neither be governed nor explained by the traditional morality. It cannot be explained because what is morally wrong seems politically so effective. The politician can use all the old words—Order, Reason, Nature, God—but only as words. The outside is the same as ever it was, but internally everything is changed to a sinister sense. The perfect imitation looks like the truth, and works like the truth, and it cannot be unmasked unless by God's intervention. In bringing up the problem of the true and the seeming-true the machiavel posed a dilemma which obsessed Shakespeare for fifteen years.

In the second tetralogy Shakespeare sees through the pietistic pretensions of the Tudor claims. Ruefully, however, he accepts the need for order-at-any-price which is its main doctrine. The machiavel is submitted to a process of whitewashing. He becomes the Bastard—the New Man proper. Falconbridge is more than half-way from Richard Crookback, the diabolical machiavel, to Prince Hal, the machiavel of goodness. Rebellion is unwise as well as wicked. The King needs first to be strong: goodness is relegated to a second place. In the conjunction of Hal and Falstaff we see the full symbolization of Elizabeth's regime. The two together represent the broken medieval unity, the partnership of Authority and Appetite; Burleigh and Walsingham and Drake and Raleigh, Ulysses and Nestor and Achilles and Ajax; wit and beef-wit, mind and body.

The third stage in Shakespeare's thought on the problem extends from *Julius Caesar* to *King Lear*. The final outcome of Shakespeare's thought is to reject both the Tudor pretensions to righteousness and the Tudor plea (on grounds of policy) for order at any price. The Tudor conception of order was both a coarsening and a distortion of the medieval. For the Middle Ages order had to be first metaphysical and moral. It was mediated into the political realm only when the spiritual requirements had been fulfilled. The main requirement was that the king in fact should be also a King in nature. Shakespeare in his third phase returns to the medieval position. The machiavel enthroned in the later Histories is finally dethroned. The Kingly nature can be machiavellian in no sense. The machiavel returns to his original role of villain, the politician opposed to Kingship and to the Nature which supports it. At the same time the machiavel is not made a melodramatic puppet. He continues to be a living and vital study of the New Man. His metaphysical and political implications, however, are as sinister as any that attached to Crookback.

I think that in the end Shakespeare solved the puzzle set by the machiavel, the puzzle of the truth and the perfect imitation of the truth. After his attempt to make the good man master of the machiavel in the same line of craft he came to the conclusion that this was neither possible nor desirable. I think that it was in the plays that the full discovery was made. An independent record of it, however, is preserved also in the *Sonnets*. *Sonnet* 124 is evidence too valuable to omit. It has direct relevance, too, for the understanding of what Edgar and Cordelia mean:

> If my dear love were but the child of state,
> It might for Fortune's bastard be unfather'd,
> As subject to Time's love, or to Time's hate,
> Weeds among weeds, or flowers with flowers gather'd.
> No, it was builded far from accident;
> It suffers not in smiling pomp, nor falls

Under the blow of thralled discontent
Whereto the inviting time the fashion calls:
It fears not policy, that heretic,
Which works on leases of short-number'd hours,
But all alone stands hugely politic,
That it nor grows with heat, nor drowns with showers.
  To this I witness call the fools of Time,
  Which die for goodness, who have liv'd for crime.

The machiavel, Shakespeare realized, was bound to succeed in the sphere of 'Time'. Richard Crookback failed but that was in accordance with Hall's schema for the Divine Comedy of history. Shakespeare came to doubt that God would intervene politically except through Nature and Reason. Cordelia's survival in the tug and scamble of practical affairs cannot be guaranteed. This constitutes the main difference between the thought of the tragic period and that of the earlier Chronicles.

Shakespeare, however, never hesitates between Edmund and Cordelia. As the *Sonnet* suggests, the sphere of the 'fools of Time' is one thing and that in which Shakespeare's election is rooted quite another. Cordelia, like Shakespeare's 'dear love', transcends the temporal. We should misinterpret Cordelia's defeat if we ignored the distinction Shakespeare sets up between 'Time' and truth.

Furthermore, there is in *King Lear* the successful grand strategy of what Edgar calls 'ripeness', and Lear and Gloster 'patience': the Christian patience of *A Most Spiritual and Precious Pearl*. This, too,

fears not policy, that heretic,
Which works on leases of short-number'd hours,
But all alone stands hugely politic.

This 'ripeness' is the wisdom that wears out packs and sects of great ones. It is not limited to 'the bank and shoal of time'. It is like that meekness which shall inherit the earth, a combination of the serpent and the dove.

The preceding chapters, finally, have put forward a thesis concerning Shakespeare's thought on society. It has been argued that Shakespeare began by seeing a new thrustful godlessness attacking the pious medieval structure represented by the good King Henry VI. Regretfully, Shakespeare then comes to terms with 'the times' such as he saw them to be under Elizabeth. Last, he recognized the iniquity of the times and of the machiavel's rule. To these he opposed the society that Lear's and Gloster's prayers demand, a transcendent society adequated to the necessity for a community of goodness in which Lear's regeneration and Cordelia's truth might be completed: a Utopia and a New Jerusalem.

All these issues we have separated out Shakespeare kept together. Each being in reciprocal relation to the others no single one can stand alone. The means whereby Shakespeare handles them together is simple enough. Taken together they form a story, and the story is treated in the terms of the new organ of thought—the Elizabethan Chronicle play. At each stage of Shakespeare's thought it is the same story with which he is concerned: a story capable of changing its meanings, capable of growing as Shakespeare grows, capable of expanding its significance until in the end it becomes a parable. Throughout the tragedies that are chronicles and the chronicles that are tragedies there is only the one story. It is the story, apparently, of Killing the King. But this story, too, is merely the Elizabethan costume for the universal theme which, in the section following, we shall attempt to define further.

It is this story and its unfolding implications as Shakespeare dwells on it that provides, I think, the 'key to Shakespeare's consciousness' which Mr. T. S. Eliot was asking for in the early 'thirties. It has been missed for so long for reasons only too apparent when we read Shakespeare criticism. Criticism, after Coleridge, was only interested in 'character'. This tended to disintegrate the Chronicle statement. Atomization since Bradley has gone even further. Shakespeare's story has been broken down into separate and jarring bits: 'themes', 'world-views', 'ideas', even 'images'. The co-ordinating principle of story (the most primitively obvious one) has been overlooked. So the intention of these chapters, in part, has been to suggest a new method of approaching Shakespeare's plays, and one which will enable us to find Shakespeare's deepest meanings precisely where they should be in successful art—on the surface.

For *King Lear* is highly successful art, as efficient in expression as it is in the full communication of what it has to express. Mr. Middleton Murry, after almost laying his hand on the main clue to Shakespeare's meaning, went on to say that *King Lear* is the only play in which Shakespeare is out of his depth. The main reason which Mr. Murry gives for this opinion is the apparently compulsive surge of anti-sexual mania in Lear's mad speeches. Maybe, too, the violence of the Thunder and the wild yet calculated cruelties of the daughters added their weight. And it is easy to respond to the violences of word and act in *King Lear* as if they were mere expressions of the chaos of 'a confuse mixture'. It is easy not to see the containing frame in which the violence and the cruelty are firmly held: that frame of Nature ascending from the unthinkable up to the ungraspable, with Cordelia the apex of the pyramid, a still and lucent quiet of thought, the point at which we 'rush into natural theology'.

Shakespeare's 'terrifying clairvoyance . . . leads toward, and is only completed by, the religious comprehension.' This is a less clumsy phrasing of the same final distinction which Miss Ellis-Fermor wishes to make: 'Tragedy is an interim reading of life.' Miss Ellis-Fermor contends that tragedy falls short of the full religious expression, that tragedy balances the 'religious' reading of life against the 'unreligious' reading. On so large a question it is possible only to dogmatize. The 'balance' Miss Ellis-Fermor might have had in mind is, in *King Lear* for example, the counterpoise of Cordelia and the Thunder —this latter understood as a sub-humanity. There is this counterpoise in the play. I cannot feel, however, that one fits into one 'reading' of life, and the other into an opposed 'reading' of life. Both are parts of a unified experience, both belong to a unitary apprehension of life. Both, I think, are animated and unified by the choice they activate. Tragedy is not an interim reading of life, nor does it hesitate, I think, between two rival attitudes to life. Miss Ellis-Fermor has been misled here by the tradition in which modern criticism writes—the tradition, particularly, that has received and inherited Arnold's original distortions. Tragedy presents us with a single and unifying experience. A 'view of life' by comparison with such an experience is inanimate, irrelevant, or partial.

Mr. Eliot's phrase includes the admirably descriptive word 'clairvoyance'. It, too, however, seems to set tragic clairvoyance against religious insight, Shakespeare's presumed non-Christian attitude against the attitudes of orthodox faith. I do not myself believe that there is a necessary contradiction between tragic vision and religious vision—though some tragedies can be irreligious as some religions can be non-tragic. Shakespeare, I feel certain, was thoroughly imbued with the very finest spirit of Elizabethan Christianity. In his case tragic clairvoyance and Christian perception are not mutually exclusive modes of vision. In any case a religion which contemplated good and evil clairvoyantly could hardly take any other than a tragic view. Such a religion might even be forced to find the full expression of its view, its awareness of the tragic tension and the tragic choice and the tragic unity, in dramatic form. In this sense, then, I am inclined to regard Mr. Eliot's distinction as slightly unreal. For if by 'the completion of the religious comprehension' is meant the full completion of that experience, in beatific ecstasy, then not only is the tragic clairvoyance capable of completion by this, but so also is any religious experience that falls short of final beatitude. To me, certainly, the clairvoyance of *King Lear* is hardly distinguishable from religious insight. It is not only our profoundest tragedy; it is also our profoundest expression of an essentially Christian comment on man's world and his society, using the terms and benefitting by the formulations of the Christian tradition. *King Lear*, I feel, is at least as Christian as the *Divine Comedy*. And it is less open to the suspicion of using its righteousness like a savage. Its gifts are those of gentleness, compassion, and truth: patience and charity.

PART III

THE POET'S SOCIETY

THE POET'S SOCIETY

Like all the other books on Shakespeare this book has at-
tempted to tell the truth about Shakespeare for the first time.
Truth, I believe, is what the poet intends. It is this which makes
the great and successful poet rank with the saint. It is this, too,
which gives the great poet his relevance to times not his own:
for all men at all times betray an interest in the truth. I should
like, now, to tease out some of the implications of poetry regarded as truth, poetry regarded as having some permanence of
appeal.

The most important thing for criticism to decide is exactly
how it understands 'universality': how, in our case, it understands what Ben Jonson said about Shakespeare:

> He was not of an age, but for all time.

I propose to approach 'universality' first by way of the history
of some literary-critical concepts used to explain it, and then
by way of ethics generally—a field in which, I think, the literary
problem occurs again in essentially the same pattern. This will
make possible, I hope, some re-statement of the ancient platitude
that the poet is also the good man. It will reinforce, too, what I
regard as the central truth of *King Lear*: the truth, namely, that
the good man needs a community of goodness. It will enable us,
I hope, to define the universal theme (there can be only one)—
that theme which every man and every age has to work out, and
which the art that is universal is peculiarly concerned with; the

theme that finds its fullest expression in *King Lear* but which we can sense behind practically every story that maintains, so puzzlingly for the most part, a permanent hold on our minds when our minds are most fully extended: the theme of the poet and his society, or, more specifically, the theme of the Good Man in the Bad Society.

[I]

ROMANTIC CRITICISM AND ETERNAL NATURE

'The latest generations of men will find new meanings in Shakespeare, new elucidations of their own human being.' Few people will quarrel with Carlyle here. Carlyle insists, as Jonson insisted, that Shakespeare is not only an Elizabethan. Later generations do find new meanings in Shakespeare. They go to him continually for 'new elucidations of their own human being'. Shakespeare is the greatest of our contemporaries.

Carlyle explained how this comes about in terms of two fundamental romantic concepts: the idea that the poet is not fully aware of all that he is in fact doing, and the idea that he is merely a channel for truth wider than he can consciously embrace:

There is more in Shakespeare's intellect than we have yet seen. It is what I call an unconscious intellect: there is more virtue in it than he himself is aware of. . . . Shakespeare's Art is not Artifice; the noblest worth of it is not there by plan or pre-contrivance. It grows up from the deeps of Nature, through the noble sincere soul who is the voice of Nature.

For Carlyle 'unconscious intellect' means that the work of art *grows*: 'It grows up from the deeps of Nature through the noble and prophetic soul who is the voice of Nature'. We are here, of course, in the strong main current of romantic thought. Behind Carlyle is Coleridge and Burke. Expressing itself through him is the mood that has been analysed as both conservative and utopian. The romantic stands before what *is*: in Burke's case the British Constitution, in Coleridge's the numinous primrose, in Carlyle's Shakespeare's art. He sees this as a phenomenal actuality dense with the meanings of all that non-existence finally embodied here and now and in this thing: all the past, all the potential, all the ideal suddenly become present, actual, and real —an existence.

The romantic frame of mind is a continuing possibility. Before the great work of art particularly we do have a strong sense of inevitability and 'this-ness'. We can follow the romantics, too, in not setting over narrow limits to the situation in which the work of art belongs. In any creative activity the artist co-operates with circumstance. Where everything is moving at the same speed and in the same direction he may not be aware of his own drift. In certain circumstances, even, the theme will choose the man rather than the man the theme. Shakespeare's *King Lear*, for example, is an old play, and before that a folk-tale, when he comes to it. Yet when he comes to it the story seems the inevitable corner-stone to his work over sixteen years: something to which he has been moving since *Henry VI, Part I*. Again, the play requires the company, the company the theatre, around the theatre the town, and acting through the town all the motives, purposes, and wishes of an age. The play belongs to a time. Part of the 'unconscious intellect' is not even in Shakespeare's head. So far we can follow the romantics' thought in comfort.

But even while we think we are following, it is easy to deviate. To admit that 'silent growth' shares in the production of a work of art is one thing. For us, however, to think of Shakespeare's co-operating circumstance is to think of *history*, with all its various factors, its conditioning influences, trends and traditions, currents of life and thought carrying the artist along. And this is not the romantic view of what a thing *is*; this is not the wondering romantic passiveness before the object.

Carlyle meant by Nature everything that we mean by History

except that which we regard as the essentially historical: that which makes one time different from another. Even his historical biographies are studies in this history-less Nature. Carlyle's Nature is our History minus the idea of meaningful change. It is a timeless realm from which phenomena precipitate themselves into time. It spills over with events; it is a realm of activity, meaning, and ceaseless turmoil, but not the organized continuum we think of as History. Coleridge can explain Carlyle most clearly. On the subject of Shakespeare's universality Coleridge writes:

Whilst the poet registers what is past, he projects the future in a wonderful degree, and makes us feel, however slightly, and see, however dimly, the state of being in which there is neither past nor future, but all is permanent in the very energy of nature. . . . [Shakespeare] is of no age . . . the body and substance of his works comes out of the unfathomable depths of his oceanic mind: his observation and reading, which was considerable, supplied him with the drapery of his figures.

The image of 'the drapery' and 'the figures' we shall come across later. Here we shall merely repeat that to say Shakespeare is of no age, but belongs to all times, must be in some sense admitted. We can apply the notion immediately to Shakespeare criticism. There are some who make the Elizabethan audience the final arbiter in matters of Shakespeare interpretation. It is useful to remember that we do not know how the Elizabethan audience regarded their entertainer. Nor would it be necessarily helpful if we did. Coleridge is right when he points out that in all likelihood Shakespeare was no more fully understood in his own age than he has been by any other. Even if we knew the Elizabethans' reaction their appreciation would in no way guarantee ours. Nor could their judgments assist in the evaluations we should still have to make for ourselves.

The romantic stands before whatever *is*. Keat's phrase for the attitude is 'negative capability'. There is something peculiarly negative in the ability to see every object, equally with any other, as an expression of the 'All'. Romantic philosophy,

Coleridge asserts, begins and ends in wonder. It begins so with the question, 'How did this come to be?' It ends even more so, in an augmented awe: 'This has come to be through a whole universe of energy issuing into a particular here and now'. Carlyle gives us the same overwhelming thought with his own inflated gusto:

But indeed that strange outbudding of our whole English existence, which we call the Elizabethan Era, did it too come of its own accord? The 'Tree Igdrasil' buds and withers by its own laws—too deep for our scanning. Yet it does bud and wither, and every bough and leaf of it is thereby fixed eternal laws; not a Sir Thomas Lucy but comes at the hour fixed for him. Curious, I say, and not sufficiently considered: how everything does co-operate with all; not a leaf rotting in the highway but is indissoluble portion of solar and stellar systems; no thought, word or act of man but has sprung withal out of all men! It is all a Tree: circulation of sap and influences, mutual communication of every minutest leaf with the lowest talon of a root, with every other greatest and minutest portion of the whole. The Tree Igdrasil, that has its roots down in the Kingdom of Hela and Death, whose boughs overspread the highest Heaven!

Nature, then, is the hinterland of phenomena. It is an unhistorical ferment of meaning and life, constantly throwing up the concrete forms in which it expresses itself. Or it is a vast ramification of organic interconnections, the Tree Igdrasil, whose smallest leaf communicates with roots in the Kingdom of Hela. This is the Nature of which Shakespeare is the voice. It is this which gives his work universality. For we, like Sir Thomas Lucy, are parts of the Tree. Our connection with Shakespeare is through the roots in the Kingdom of Hela.

We may not adopt the whole romantic theory as the romantics themselves state it. Romantic criticism is still, however, the best criticism we have of Shakespeare. The sense for the immediate timeless object in which 'all-ness' finds a focus, and the sense for the organic, the interconnected, and the unified, goes over into this criticism. It leads Coleridge, for example, to expound the profundities of a single poetic image, or to demonstrate how the whole of Shakespeare's work differs from the whole of Massinger's, Shakespeare creating unities where Massinger makes mere assemblages.

[II]

SHAKESPEARIAN DRAMA AND ELIZABETHAN NATURE

While we need Shakespeare to be our own contemporary we do not need, therefore, the romantic Nature, too. We might look instead at a Shakespearean comment on Nature and the artist's role. It is not going too far to see Shakespeare's advice to an actor as embodying a view of the dramatist's craft more generally:

> . . . anything so overdone is from the purpose of Playing, whose end both at the first and now, was and is, to hold as 'twer the Mirrour up to Nature; to show Vertue her owne Feature, Scorne her owne Image, and the verie Age and Bodie of the Time, his forme and pressure.
>
> (Hamlet, II, ii).

One thing is clear from Shakespeare's words. His conception is entirely different from that of the romantics. To hold a mirror up to their Nature would produce no image.

Apart from this the interpretation of the passage cannot be absolutely certain. Shakespeare's phrase might mean that art ought to produce faithful photographs. A more likely meaning, I think, would make Nature here fit in with the Nature we have already examined in connection with Hooker and Bacon. Art, that is, should trace the clear outlines of some eternal Nature, a Nature however which is the storehouse of forms clear enough and definite enough to be seen in the mirror. Looking in the mirror of art Virtue then will see her proper feature, the ridiculous and contemptible be recognized for what they are. Art is a magic mirror which tells the real truth.

What are the 'forme and pressure' which the 'Age and Bodie of the Time' is shown? It may be that here again art is a passive wax on which the historical actualities must leave their imprint.

Again, however, it is tempting to see in Shakespeare's words the technical meanings of the *Novum Organum*:

> God, the bestower and creator of forms. . . . The form of heat and light . . . means no more than the law of heat and light. . . . There is no small difference between the idols of the human mind and the ideas of the Divine mind—that is to say, between certain idle dogmas and *the real signatures and impressions on created things as they are found in actual experience.*

By an 'impression' (Shakespeare's 'pressure') Bacon means that there is something already precisely formed behind the phenomena we see so regularly shaped. By 'form' he means the eternal law rather than the empirical manifestation. Shakespeare might conceivably mean the same thing.

By 'forme and pressure' I understand Shakespeare to be implying the operative actualities that order his contemporary society. There can be no ambiguity over this at least: Shakespeare conceives his drama as having a direct contemporary reference. By conscious intent the chronicle play deals with the Elizabethan age not with some timeless realm of energy. It fits in more with our own view of History than with Carlyle's Nature. Shakespeare himself is fully conscious of what is meant by being up-to-date:

> For he is but a bastard to the time,
> That does not smack of observation.

The Nature of the *Hamlet* passage means, then, in some sense a current actuality, and maybe, behind this, the divine forms that account for it. Unlike that of the Romantics, the Elizabethan Nature is never in any danger of usurping God's position, nor of losing precision and manifoldness of outline. Elizabethan Nature is a tidy servant, 'God's handmaid'. Her house is recognizable for having everything in its place. The patterned distinctness of things is emphasized rather than the Igdrasil infinitude of inter-relations. Each object stands in its special place on its particular shelf of 'degree'. Two relations define it: the relation to next above, and the relation to next below. 'Negative capability'—the Romantic gift for leaving your place and finding yourself in that of something else—is thus impossible. One's nature depends on one's position. The complete serial order of these positions constitutes Nature. Position also defines disposition, 'the peculiar disposition appropred unto (things) by God their creatour'. To quit this position and this order is to move into the sphere not of the meaningful and indeterminate energy, but into Chaos. This, at any rate, is how Sir Thomas Elyot sees it:

Moreover, take away ordre from all thynges what shulde then remayne? Certes nothynge finally, except some men wolde imagine eftsones *Chaos*: which of some is expound a confuse mixture.

[III]

LITERATURE AND THE ROMANTIC IDEA

Our problem now is to find a means of combining the idea of Shakespeare interpreting his own time and the idea of his interpreting that also which is useful to ours.

There are two formulae which have been devised to meet the situation. One is the liberal view of Matthew Arnold which depends on the liberal view of an idea. The other is the romantic view of Arnold's forerunners which depends on the romantic conception of what an idea is, and how poetry offers us just such ideas. Both of these we might now look at, before turning to the field of ethics in which the problems reappear.

The reaction against Coleridge and Carlyle maintained (as Sir Thomas Elyot would) that romantic Nature is, in fact, merely 'a confuse mixture'. Nothing could be less intellectual or more indefinite than a romantic 'idea'. After Coleridge and Carlyle the development is to people the timeless realm with 'ideas' of another kind. Coleridge, for example, had called

Shakespeare the most philosophical of poets—philosophical in the romantic sense. Matthew Arnold begins also to talk about 'high poetic seriousness'. But this rapidly makes poetry into a 'criticism of life', and this criticism the 'application of profound ideas to life'. And Arnold now conceives of ideas as abstract formulations, generalizations, partial systematizations, philosophical dogmas predominantly intellectual in form. And this makes way for the drama which handles theses about life, and for the modern criticism which hunts its themes through Shakespeare's work.

Arnold's conception is neither the Elizabethan nor the romantic 'idea'. It is not the Elizabethan because for the Elizabethan the 'forms' still remain actual phenomena regarded in their structural aspect. It is not the romantic, because for the romantic an idea is not exclusively an intellectual generalization but a particular state of being; it is that which is given to (or should we say made by?) the whole man interacting with his universe. Where ideas for the liberal tradition of the nineteenth century are forms of Thought, ideas for the Elizabethans and the romantics are forms of Being.

Thus the romantic idea is a poem, and the poem is life. There is nothing outside the idea which it could be applied to. Poetry is all that we know and all that we know with when we know. It is the 'sacred river'. The greatest of the romantic poems about life and nature and art—itself a 'huge fragment'— tells us as much as we can know about it:

> And from this chasm, with ceaseless turmoil seething,
> As if the earth in fast thick pants were breathing,
> A mighty fountain momently was forced:
> Amid whose swift half-intermitted burst
> Huge fragments vaulted like rebounding hail,
> Or chaffy grain beneath the thresher's flail:
> And 'mid these dancing rocks at once and ever
> It flung up momently the sacred river.
> Five miles meandering with a mazy notion
> Through wood and dale the sacred river ran,

Then reached the caverns measureless to man,
And sank in tumult to a lifeless ocean:
And 'mid this tumult Kubla heard from far
Ancestral voices prophesying war!

Kubla Khan is the kind of poem to which Arnold's formula cannot be applied. Yet it is a great and a profound poem. Poetry,
I believe, does represent a wholeness of being that we cannot
find in the application of liberal ideas to life. What the greatest
poetry gives us seems to answer more to the romantic 'idea'—
a full state of being in which the mind achieves that kind of
order which allows of clearer perceptions. Poetry, as Blake said,
cleanses the doors of perception. It expresses the 'whole man' in
a way that ideas as Arnold understood them cannot possibly do.

The distinction might be put in this way.—Ideas as abstract
formulations belong to a wider context than they themselves
can indicate. In itself the idea is meaningless. What gives it
meaning is the power and insight of the mind that uses it. The
romantic idea is Arnold's idea properly placed in its context of
such power: ideas so disposed in their context of experience that
the idea is never given without the wisdom to use it being given
too. Truths, as Wordsworth said, must be carried alive into the
heart: by poems.

The level at which wisdom operates with the ideas given to it
is one thing. The level at which the intellect forms its abstractions is another. It does not follow, of course, that poetry must
reject the intellect's abstractions. They are, on the contrary,
necessary instruments. Great poetry will operate with great
generalizations. We might almost say indeed that great poetry
will be impossible without great generalizations. It is merely
that the two must not be confused, and, especially, that the
proper relation between them should not be reversed. Criticism,
because of its method, always tends to reverse this order. It must
talk, very often, as if poems were merely the applications of
profound ideas to life. At his best the critic should be content
to point silently to the great works in a significant order. As

soon, however, as he breaks silence, he will suggest the formulae he judges to be appropriate, and which he hopes will also be helpful: will help others to such an experience of the poem as he himself has had. All life, Keats wrote, is an Allegory. There is a human compulsion to provide the Allegory with a title. The title stands to the Allegory as the profound idea to life.

A poem, I should say, then, achieves universality when it is the expression of a certain human wholeness. It makes contact with us at the level of its wisdom rather than its formulations. So Shakespeare is contemporary with us. At the same time, the great poet like Shakespeare must interpret the 'very age and body' of his own generation. The great insights are insights into what is happening in history.

[IV]

THE POET AND THE GOOD MAN

The distinction between the romantics' 'idea' and Arnold's, between wisdom and generalizations, between the poet's wholeness and the history on which he brings that wholeness to bear, is the crucial distinction which gives our common life its peculiar and fearful tension: the distinction between the spirit of the law and the letter. The poet's dilemma is our common dilemma more clearly realized. We shall understand the Poet more readily therefore, if we understand the Good Man. For goodness, like poetry, is a kind of wholeness.

In any piece of ethical conduct there would seem to be at least three different spheres brought into relation. First there is our own private consciousness and our willed intention. Second, there are all those circumstances which seem 'given', which we were born into, are surrounded by, have to deal with. Finally, there is a third element involved. This stands over against our private consciousness as something definitely objective and real: it is, in fact, that kind of truth which is more important than our own life.

It stands over against the sphere of circumstance and history, too. It is not real as circumstances are. It is, in fact, a criticism and an assessment of those circumstances. Insisting on its own realization, it demands a change in them. It is, therefore, neither subjective like our private world, nor objective like the public world. It is in this sphere that the 'spirit' of the law exists, along with all such notions as truth, justice, charity, and freedom. The 'letter' always falls short of this sphere, along with all codes, schemes, attitudes to life, and all pharisee-isms whatever.

It is fatally easy to lose one's way between the spirit and the letter and the letter and the spirit. A failure of intellect or a failure of energy, and tired everyman will content himself with the grim overlordship of some code. The most compelling statement of the plight that then ensues is Blake's address *To The Accuser who is the God of This World*:

> Truly, My Satan, thou art but a Dunce,
> And dost not know the Garment from the Man.
> Every Harlot was a Virgin once,
> Nor canst thou ever change Kate into Nan.
>
> Tho' thou art Worship'd by the Names Divine
> Of Jesus and Jehovah, thou art still
> The Son of Morn in weary Night's decline,
> The lost Traveller's Dream under the Hill.

For Blake the Truth is a man. It is inseparable from the idea of personality. The codes and categories are 'garments'. Universality is possible because the same truth can wear at different times the different draperies. The truth is what Mr. T. S. Eliot would call the tradition, and the garment the experiment. Wholeness in action will inevitably mean action in the frame that is given, and action on the time that surrounds the agent. But the same wholeness always involves the third realm which stands over against both the intentional man and the body of his time. And this third realm of truth is in some sense timeless. At any rate, it is not intrinsically easier to avoid mistakes in judging our contemporary Kate or Nan than it is to avoid misinterpreting Shakespeare. Like Kate and Nan, Shakespeare, too, is our neighbour.

The three spheres brought into relation in the moral act are the three spheres we need in criticism to explain universality. The theory of moral goodness as wholeness, and of great poetry also as being an expression of the whole man, obviously leads to the convergence of ethics and poetry.

The view that the poet is the good man has been, in fact, the longest held of any. It is in Shakespeare's contemporary Ben Jonson:

For if men will impartially, and not asquint, look toward the office and function of a poet, they will easily conclude to themselves the impossibility of any man's being a good poet without first being a good man. He that is said to be able to inform young men to all good disciplines, inflame grown men to all great virtues, keep old men in their best and supreme state, or, as they incline to childhood, recover them to their first strength; that comes forth the interpreter and arbiter of nature, a teacher of things divine no less than human, a master in manners; and can alone, or with few, effect the business of mankind: this, I take him, is no subject for pride and ignorance to exercise their railing rhetoric upon.

It is, of course, in Carlyle, too. Shakespeare's morality consists in 'that calm creative perspicacity of Shakespeare':

No *twisted*, poor convex-concave mirror, reflecting all objects with its own convexities and concavities; a perfectly *level* mirror;— that is to say withal, if we will understand it, a man justly related to all things and men, a good man.

It is above all in Coleridge:

I have often thought that religion (speaking of it only as it accords with poetry, without reference to its more serious impressions) is the poetry of mankind, both having for their objects: To generalize our notions; to prevent men from confining their attention solely, or

chiefly, to their own narrow sphere of action, and to their own individual circumstances. By placing them in certain awful relations it
merges the individual man in the whole species, and makes it impossible for any one man to think of his future lot, or indeed of his present condition, without at the same time comprising in his view his
fellow creatures—we need not wonder that it has pleased Providence
that the divine truths of religion should have been revealed to us in
the form of poetry; and that at all times poets, not the slaves of any
particular sectarian opinions, should have joined to support all those
delicate sentiments of the heart (often when they were most opposed
to the reigning philosophy of the day) which may be called the feeding
streams of religion.

Coleridge's view is similar, I think, to what I have suggested.
The 'certain awful relations' in which man is placed are those
of common experience, the relation to history and the relation
to truth and the dilemma of spirit and letter. Imagination does
not have to fake its world. Its task is to see the world. It operates
with the sum of the awful relations which are constitutive of
man: consciousness, history, truth; myself, my neighbour, God.
The territories of poetry and goodness overlap: Jesus, as Blake
said, was an Artist.

Great poetry expresses the whole man in one way, as ethical
choice does in another. Great poetry, therefore, has common
ground with true morality. Poetic insight is also moral insight.
Because art is human it is ethical, because it is ethical it is political, and because it is political it assesses, judges, and illuminates
its time. We are like Shakespeare in being human:

> Shakespeare is the only biographer of Shakespeare; and even he can
> tell nothing except to the Shakespeare in us; that is to our most appre-
> hensive and sympathetic hour.

We have not the same wholeness as Shakespeare, but a share in
the same wholeness: we go to him still for 'new elucidations of
our own human being'.

Shakespeare, however, needs the reader as much as the reader
needs him. The utopian intention of art is to illuminate choice

and also to activate choice. Its aim is to communicate truth, and this aim the audience, reader, or critic, can further or frustrate. The relation between reader and writer in all art that touches the universal is a relationship therefore of complete equality and freedom. This is as apparent in Blake's poem on Satan as it is in Shakespeare's *King Lear*. Neither presents us with an 'attitude to life': that is the post-romantic perversion of what the romantics meant by poetry needing to be 'philosophical'. In both Shakespeare and Blake we feel that the writer is moving freely over a field of truth: he is considering facts. The reader is free to accompany, to reconsider, to accept or reject; but he has no sense of compulsion from the writer's design on his allegiances. Universal art illuminates choice and activates it. It would frustrate itself by any intention to dictate choice. The very greatest poetry, therefore, can be recognized by its tonal relationship. In such poetry as *King Lear* or *Songs of Innocence* there is a complete absence of anxiety. The poetry is paradisal.

[V]

THE POET'S SOCIETY

Blake said Jesus was an Artist. He also said, Empire is against Art. Western society is not in accordance with the purposes of either good man or poet, nor does it fit the real nature of Kate and Nan. It is for this reason that Lear's prayer on the Heath (echoing the cry that Jack Kett had raised in 1549, and anticipating the cry to come in 1649 from Winstanley and the Diggers) is so central to Shakespeare's inspiration. It is not that the universal poet is necessarily a socialist. It is, rather, that socialism is the effort by persons not poets to translate into action the insights the poet wins from his criticism of society. The nemesis of successful socialism will be an anti-socialist poetry. For the essence of art is anarchic. Art is the criticism of politics. The poet's politics are the politics of the next jump ahead. The poet is the Good Man in the Bad Society.

The Good Man in the Bad Society is the title, too, I think, of the universal theme. Common life and the life of art are shaped by the same tensions. The title of the universal theme is the title, therefore, of the Allegory Keats said all life is. And *King Lear* I see as the fullest statement which Western art has provided both of the Allegory and of the universal theme.

What is Allegory in life is story in Art. *King Lear* is intrinsically a good story. Even as a folk-tale it is as compelling as a sermon. In Shakespeare's hands it achieves all the force of parable. To allow our eye to follow the naïve contour of the plot will carry us as far into Shakespeare's meanings as we wish to go.

The story is inclusive in scope. It brings together, merely as a plot, both the inner and the outer worlds, both what Blake called Empire and what he called Art. It shows us choice, right and wrong, between the two. It is not merely the story of a man with an awkward family. It is a story of two kinds of society. Nor does the story stop here. It goes so far as to balance any human nature whatever, and any society, against the Thunder. And the main meanings all the time are where they should be in successful art: on the surface. To get most help from Shakespeare we need to forget almost all our Shakespeare criticism, to take the things in the story and the people in the story at their face-value, and then see them in terms of the story as a whole. For the story is a parable: the parable of the poet and 'the times', of the Good Man in the Bad Society.

NOTES

Part I

p. 16   Coleridge: *The Friend*, Essay XV. Bohn edition, p. 65.

p. 21   Bacon: *Advancement of Learning*. Bohn edition, p. 100–101.

p. 23   Bacon: op cit., p. 101–102

p. 24   Hooker: *Ecclesiastical Polity*. Everyman edition, p. 159.

p. 26   Hooker: op. cit., p. 176–7, 178.

p. 28   A. E. Housman: *Collected Poems*, p. 65.
      'Wanderers eastward, wanderers west,
       Know you why you cannot rest?
     'Tis that every mother's son
      Travails with a skeleton.'

p. 28   Hooker: op. cit., p. 188–9.

p. 30   *Homily against Excess of Apparel:*
     'Certainly such as delight in gorgeous apparel are commonly puffed up with pride and filled with divers vanities.'

p. 30   Hooker: op. cit., p. 184.

p. 32   Bacon: op. cit., p. 103.

p. 33   Hooker: *Sermon on the Certainty and Perpetuity of Faith in the Elect*. Works. Clarendon edition, II, p. 589.

p. 33   Bacon: *Confession of Faith*.

p. 34   *Bestiary*. E. E. T. S., Vol. 49, p. 16.

p. 34   L. Andrewes: *Collection of Posthumous and Orphan Lectures*. Published 1657.

p. 35   Fuller: *The Holy and the Profane State*. Ed. Jas. Nichols, p. 357–8.

p. 37   Coverdale: *Works of Bp. Coverdale: Fruitful Lessons: etc.* Ed. Parker Society, p. 502.

p. 37   Hutchinson: *Works*. Ed. Parker Society, p. 78.

p. 37   Spenser: Globe edition, p. 609.

p. 39   Hobbes: *Leviathan*. Ed. H. Morley, p. 52.

p. 39   Hobbes: op. cit., p. 63.

p. 39   Hobbes: op. cit., p. 64.

p. 47   Hobbes: op. cit., p. 154.

p. 49   The Grand Lease. See 'The Bishopric of Durham and Capitalist Reformation', by H. R. Trevor-Roper. *Durham University Journal,* Vol. XXXVIII, No. 2.

p. 51   G. R. Owst. See *Literature and Pulpit in Mediaeval Preaching.*

p. 51   *The Third Part of the Homily against Disobedience and Wilful Rebellion.*

p. 52   Hooker: op. cit., p. 188.

Part II

p. 58   E. M. W. Tillyard. See *Shakespeare's History Plays.*

p. 66   *The Mirror for Magistrates.* Ed. Lily B. Campbell.

p. 82   E. M. W. Tillyard: op. cit.

p. 82   J. D. Wilson. See *The Fortunes of Falstaff.*

p. 92   Coleridge: *Lectures on Shakespeare.* Bohn edition, p. 487–8.

p. 95   A. C. Bradley. See 'The Rejection of Falstaff', *Oxford Lectures on Poetry,* p. 262–3.

p. 96   E. M. W. Tillyard: op. cit.

p. 97   Winstanley: *The New Law of Righteousness—Works.* Ed. G. H. Sabine, p. 202.

    'Now whereas the Creation, Man, should live in equalitie one towards another; this A-dam hath lifted up mountaines and hils of oppressing powers, and there by that, damned and stopped up that universal communitie: Therefore at the first rising up of this serpentine power to enslave the Creation, he might well be declared by way of lamentation A-dam Adam.'

p. 97   J. D. Wilson: op. cit.

p. 114   Johnson: *Johnson and Shakespeare.* Ed. Walter Raleigh, p. 161–2.

    'If my sensations could add anything to the general suffrage, I might relate, that I was many years ago so shocked by *Cordelia's* death, that I know not whether I ever endured to read again the last scenes of the play till I undertook to revise them as an editor.'

p. 115   Coleridge: op. cit., p. 335.

p. 115   A. W. Schlegel: *Schlegel on Dramatic Art.* Bohn edition, p. 413.

p. 115   H. Ulrici: *Shakespeare's Dramatic Art,* p. 197–8.

p. 115   Dr. J. Bucknill: *The Mad Fold of Shakespeare,* 2nd edition, p. 174–5.

p. 116   Becon: *Works*. Ed. Parker Society, p. 87.

p. 117   Chaucer: *The Clerkes Tale*. For fuller treatment of the parallel between Cordelia and Griselde see my article referred to below in note to p. 135.

p. 117   *A Little Boy Lost*. I am indebted to Dr. J. Bronowski for first drawing my attention to the similarity between this poem and the situation in the partition scene.

p. 119   Dante. See note to p. 131.

p. 119   Winstanley: op. cit. Addressing the professional priests, Winstanley writes: 'Read the Record, and let Reason judge, whether you find the power of prayer so customarily in you, or whether it be not covetousness in you to get a temporal living that stirs you up to use this trade.'

p. 122   Dante: *The Convivio*. Temple Classics edition, note to p. 66.

p. 122   Master Ripon of Durham. See G. R. Owst, op. cit.

p. 123   H. Ulrici: op. cit., p. 202–3.

p. 125   'Which twain have brought her to.'—Only Dowden, as far as I have been able to discover, suspects that there might be a crux here. In *Shakespeare and Dramatic Tradition*, Mr. S. L. Bethell notes the reference to Christ involved in 'redeems Nature'. I think, myself, the theological reference is very apparent, and extends, as I suggest, to the 'twain' as well.

p. 126   Wordsworth: *Lucy*.

p. 127   Sonnet 66.

p. 127   Blake: *The Poetry and Prose of William Blake*. Ed. Geoffrey Keynes. Nonesuch, p. 766.

p. 129   For the financial manners of the Renaissance Prince see *Capital and Finance in the Age of the Renaissance*, by Richard Ehrenburg, p. 43.

p. 131   Dante: op. cit., p. 139 and p. 3.

p. 131   Hooker: op. cit., p. 180.

p. 132   Winstanley: *Truth Lifting up its Head Against Scandals—Works*, p. 137.

p. 135   Coverdale. For fuller treatment of Patience and its meaning for Shakespeare see my article 'King Lear and Christian Patience' in *Cambridge Journal*, Vol. I, No. 5.

p. 158   Keats: *Letters of John Keats*. Ed. M. B. Forran, Vol. I, p. 72.

p. 161   Tillyard: op. cit.

p. 171   Bacon: *Meditationes Sacrae: De Atheismo—Works*. Ed. Spedding and Heath, Vol. VII, p. 239.

p. 171   Coverdale: op. cit., p. 175.

p. 172 Coverdale: op. cit., p. 501–2.

p. 173 Coverdale: op. cit., p. 504–5.

p. 180 Wilson Knight: 'The gash becomes bigger than the thing it cuts'—*Wheel of Fire*, p. 222.

p. 184 Dante and Shakespeare—Mr. T. S. Eliot has hinted at the difference I have in mind in his Essay on Dante (p. 26):

> 'There is a relation between the various plays of Shakespeare, taken in order; and it is a work of years to venture even one individual interpretation of the pattern in Shakespeare's carpet. It is not certain that Shakespeare himself knew what it was. It is, perhaps, a larger pattern than Dante's, but the pattern is less distinct.'

p. 188 Froissart's *Chronicle*, Bk. II, Ch. 73.

p. 188 G. R. Owst: op. cit., p. 301.

p. 192 'All have offended.' See *Homilies: First Part of the Sermon of Salvation*. The translation of Romans III, 23 in the Homilies is, 'All have offended and have need of the glory of God.' The Authorized Version, of course, translates this: 'All have *sinned* and come short of the glory of God.'

p. 196 Carlyle. See note to p. 210.

p. 196 J. D. Wilson. See *The Essential Shakespeare*.

p. 197 Nicholas Breton: *Character Writings of the Seventeenth Century*. Ed. H. Morley, p. 256.

p. 202 T. S. Eliot. See *The Wheel of Fire* by Wilson Knight: Introduction by T. S. Eliot.

p. 203 J. Middleton Murry: *Shakespeare*, p. 338–9.

p. 203 Una Ellis-Fermor: *The Frontiers of Drama*, p. 147.

p. 203 T. S. Eliot. See Essay on Andrew Marvell: *Selected Essays*, p. 283.

Part III

p. 209 Jonson: *To the Memory of My Beloved Master William Shakespeare and What he hath left us.*—Jonson has a further observation pertinent to our thesis, for drawing my attention to which I have again to thank Dr. J. Bronowski. This book assumes that Shakespeare's work gives us room to turn ourselves round in. It also assumes that within it we can see Shakespeare turning himself, and finding. himself, and growing a new self in the process. Ben Jonson, who knew Shakespeare personally and loved him, was aware of the 'turn' Shakespeare's art provided for him:

'For though the poet's matter nature be,
His art doth give the fashion: and, that he
Who casts to write a living line, must sweat,
(Such as thine are) and strike the second heat
Upon the Muses' anvil; turn the same,
And himself with it, that he thinks to frame.'

p. 210   Carlyle: *The Hero as Poet.*

p. 212   Coleridge: op. cit., p. 132 and p. 541.

p. 212   Keats: *Letters of John Keats.* Ed. M. B. Forman, I, 30.

p. 213   Coleridge: op. cit., p. 104-5.

p. 213   Carlyle: Ibid.

p. 215   Bacon: Bohn edition, p. 387 and p. 474.—The passage in
         italics is my own version of Bacon's Latin: *veras signatures
         atque impressiones factas in creaturis: prout inveniuntur.*

p. 215   'God's handmaid': Sir J. Davies' *Nosce Teipsum.*

p. 216   Sir Thos. Elyot: *The Governour.* Everyman edition, p. 3 and 4.

p. 218   Blake: op. cit., p. 197.

p. 219   Keats: op. cit., II, 327:
         'A Man's life of any worth is a continual allegory, and
         very few eyes can see the Mystery of his life—a life like the
         scriptures, figurative. . . . Lord Byron cuts a figure—but he
         is not figurative—Shakespeare led a life of Allegory: his
         works are the comments on it.'
         See also J. M. Murry: *Keats and Shakespeare,* p. 115.

p. 220   Blake: op. cit., p. 763.

p. 221   Jonson: Dedication to *Volpone.* See Works, Ed. F. Cunning-
         ham, Vol. I, p. 334.

p. 221   Carlyle: Ibid.

p. 221   Coleridge: op. cit., p. 103-4.

p. 222   Blake: op. cit., p. 766.

p. 222   R. W. Emerson: essay on *Shakespeare, or the Poet in Repre-
         sentative Men.*

General Note

The quotations from *King Lear* are from the Penguin edition edited
by Prof. G. B. Harrison. For the other plays quoted I have followed the
text of the First Folio. The divergence in practice is, I think, justified.
The Penguin *Lear* is a good, recent, cheap, and fairly available text. It
includes also the scenes omitted from the *Folio*—scenes particularly
important for a full understanding of Cordelia, and certainly for my
interpretation of her.

INDEX

INDEX